P9-EMH-024

two rings

two rings

a story of love and war

Millie Werber *and*
Eve Keller

PUBLICAFFAIRS
New York

Poem on page 208 translated by Yehoshua Aizenberg

Published in the United States by PublicAffairs™,
a Member of the Perseus Books Group
All rights reserved.
Printed in the United States of America.

PublicAffairs books are available at special discounts for bulk purchases in the U.S. by corporations, institutions, and other organizations. For more information, please contact the Special Markets Department at the Perseus Books Group, 2300 Chestnut Street, Suite 200, Philadelphia, PA 19103, call (800) 810-4145, ext. 5000, or e-mail special.markets@perseusbooks.com.

Library of Congress Cataloging-in-Publication Data

Werber, Millie, 1927-
  Two rings : a story of love and war / Millie Werber and Eve Keller.—1st ed.
    p. cm.
  ISBN 978-1-61039-122-1 (hardcover : alk. paper)
  ISBN 978-1-61039-123-8 (ebook) 1. Werber, Millie, 1927- 2.
Jews—Poland—Radom—Biography. 3. Holocaust, Jewish
(1939-1945)—Poland—Radom—Personal narratives. 4. Jewish children in
the Holocaust—Poland—Radom—Biography. 5. Radom
(Poland)—Biography. I. Keller, Eve, 1960- II. Title.
  DS134.72.W44A3 2012
  940.53'18092—dc23
  [B]
                                                                2011037794

First Edition

10 9 8 7 6 5 4 3 2 1

To my dear children, grandchildren, and great-grandchildren, whom I cherish and love, and whom I could not have dared to believe I would ever have.

And to my two great loves—one that was consumed in a moment and the other that flourished for sixty years.

I want to thank my beloved sons Martin and David for urging me to tell my stories for the sake of our family and for the sake of history. I am especially grateful to Martin for bringing Eve and me together as well as for his steadfast devotion to this project throughout every stage of its development.

Deepest thanks, of course, to Eve for the enduring love and friendship we share and for managing to find the voice of my heart. Seeing myself expressed in her words is truly a wonderous gift.

—Millie Werber

To David

Best reader, best friend

—Eve Keller

Introduction

EVE KELLER

I FIRST MET MILLIE WERBER AT HER SON MARTIN'S HOUSE. He and his wife, Bracha, are family friends of mine, and once a month on Friday nights, they invite a group of twenty or more to their home to share a potluck Shabbat dinner, filled with casual conversation and song. Millie had been coming to these dinners for several years, ever since her husband Jack died in the autumn of 2006, and I had seen her, sitting quietly at the end of the table, listening, attentive, but always a little held back, an observer more than an easy participant in the boisterous goings-on. A diminutive woman, barely touching five feet tall, Millie was always impeccably dressed—a tailored dark blue dress, or perhaps a simple sweater jacket and slacks. Her clothes, like her demeanor, were graceful and quiet. We had been polite with each other, and I could tell there was a warmth to her—her eyes would brighten readily whenever she greeted the many people who came over to her—but she seemed rather reserved, and her stillness made her seem somewhat fragile, too; our interaction had never gotten far beyond the how-nice-to-see-you's.

Martin first proposed the idea of my interviewing his mother and writing a book about her wartime experiences. Though urged over the years by members of her family, Millie had been reluctant to speak in detail about her life. It can be that way with survivors, I'm told—not wanting to impose themselves on others, not wanting to burden people with the horrors of the past. But Martin thought that perhaps now, finally, Millie might be agreeable, and he thought that the two of us might hit it off. He had a feeling about us, I suppose.

I was reluctant, too, at first. I'm an academic, a professor of English literature, not a history buff and far from a Holocaust scholar. And though Jewish, my family has little connection to the traumas of the war. No one in my family died in the Holocaust. Three of my four grandparents were born in the United States; the fourth came from Hungary late in the nineteenth century. Growing up in suburban New York, I barely had any experience of anti-Semitism: When I was in high school and played violin in a county orchestra, my stand partner, a devout Catholic, asked me once if she could see my horns. But this was harmless, a parochial silliness; whatever malevolence lived in the age-old slur she had heard, none of it lived in her.

So I was tentative starting this project with Millie, because I could see no way in; there was no clear connection between Millie and me that would make such a project viable. If I had experienced nothing of real anti-Semitism, nothing of true hardship, nothing of danger or the kind of dread that keeps you awake and trembling in your bed at night, how was I to understand Millie, who was forged in these things, who was made by them and still lives them? How was I to understand the experience of what she would tell me, the *feeling* of her experience?

Nonetheless, we decided to try. We agreed that I would visit Millie regularly in her home, an elegantly appointed ranch on suburban Long Island.

"Where shall we begin?" I asked the first time. And without further prompting, the stories came pouring out. Like a dam undone, a torrent of stories, jumbled together, all intermixed. One ran readily into the next, the contours wholly unclear. After holding back for so long, it seemed, Millie wanted to tell everything. Something had been unleashed, and it was running—not wildly, not chaotically exactly, but with such profusion it was difficult to sort. I was lost in the surge, and Millie was, too, I know. Our first session lasted four hours; many hundreds more together followed.

At first our meetings were somewhat formal—the interviews were question-and-answer sessions. I reviewed the material from each session and returned to her with more questions—clarifying dates, pressing her for details, ensuring I understood to whom all the pronouns referred. Reconstructing the basic chronology proved relatively easy: September 1939, Germany invades Poland; spring 1941, two ghettos are established in an industrial city called Radom; summer 1942, the deportations begin, slave-labor factories are formed; a young girl marries; a good man is betrayed; too many die; the war grinds on. The incidents lay on the surface of memory.

But Millie's inner life was harder to find.

Millie told me many of her stories multiple times; often they seemed almost canonical in her telling—the words of the story recited nearly verbatim. It was as if her stories had crystallized, had become fixed in her memory in very specific terms. The telling was often difficult—we always sat with a box of tissues between us—but somehow, too, the immutable form of the stories seemed to work like an emotional buffer, providing some small measure of protection from the unformulated feelings beneath. Millie didn't always have ready access to these feelings, yet it was precisely these that I most wanted to know—that I most needed to know if I were to know her and give voice to the unarticulated reaches of her inner life.

To reach inward, I realized, much would be required of us both: We needed time for Millie to tell and retell her stories; we needed honesty and candor, too, and a growing, mutual trust. Above all, we needed to believe that somehow it would be possible, despite our differences, truly to know and be known by the other.

And for that we needed love.

I decided to step back and let Millie speak without much direction from me. I asked open, broad-based questions—what was on her mind that day; what had she been thinking about as she waited for me to arrive; what drifted through her thoughts as she lay in bed the night before? I didn't want to rush her; I wanted to let her mind go wherever it willed. And slowly I began to figure out the patterns underlying the associations of her memory, the emotional keystones that structure her experience of the world.

We soon started to see each other quite frequently, some days devoted to interviews, some devoted to fun. We found ourselves becoming friends—a Holocaust survivor in her early eighties, a suburban New Yorker touching fifty. We'd go to Lord & Taylor—one of Millie's favorite places—where we'd survey the recent arrivals, assessing the season's styles of cut and color. We'd stroll arm in arm through the departments—dresses, sportswear, accessories—and then take the elevator to the third-floor restaurant and eat grilled vegetable sandwiches among the white-haired ladies sitting with their shopping bags. We went to an eight-week film series on Holocaust movies from the 1940s at the Manhattan Jewish Community Center; we went to matinees on Broadway; once, we went to hear *La Traviata* at the Met in the middle of a violent snowstorm. I introduced Millie to YouTube, and we watched videos in her den—clips from the Carol Burnett and Lucille Ball shows, and Lily Tomlin playing Ernestine the Telephone Operator.

And we talked for hours, holding nothing back. Whom we have loved in our lives, how we have loved. The fire of a first kiss, and what it takes to sustain a marriage over decades. What we have wanted for ourselves, for our families; what we believe in and what we fear. What started as a series of formal interviews—"Tell me about the ghetto: Where did you live? How did you get food?"—turned into something else.

Millie now calls me the sister she never had. I demur: I'm thirty-three years younger than you, I say. Why not call me the daughter you never had? She gets the point and laughs. But she prefers sister. And that's fine with me.

༄

One day, almost a year after we started, Millie took me to her bedroom. I'd been there before—she would want to try on a new dress for me or show me what she'd be wearing to an up-coming family event. But on this day, she just asked me to sit on the settee across from the bed. She went into her walk-in closet; I could see her rummaging around in the back behind her clothes. She came out holding an accordion folder filled with old pictures and documents. I'd seen copies of most of these before—an entire wall of her spacious furnished base-ment is decorated with family pictures—some of her own chil-dren and grandchildren, most of her family from Europe. Her mother, her father, her brother, her aunt and uncle, her two cousins. Millie's aunt had retrieved the pictures after the war from friends in Paris to whom she had sent them in the 1930s.

But Millie then showed me some things I hadn't seen before—the dried, yellowed petals of a chrysanthemum, rem-nants of a flower given to her by Jack on their wedding day; a pair of gold rings, one with the initials HG engraved on a little medallion on the top of the ring; a small, tattered photograph of a young couple looking expectantly toward the camera. "My Heniek," she said, "this is my Heniek."

She gave the rings to me to look at, and then she told me what she had never spoken of before—how she had managed to save the picture and rings through the war, where she had kept them for the many decades that followed, what she did with them, secretly, throughout her life, who knew about them, and who didn't. Millie had told me much about Heniek by then, but she hadn't told me this. When I saw the look in her eyes as she held the picture out to me, her finger gently tracing the creases and ripples on its surface, I knew that here was the heart of Millie's story, that hers was not in its essence simply a survivor's story of suffering and loss, but more deeply a story of young and ardent love in the midst of the horror—in spite of the horror—and one that in some quiet way has continued unabated ever since.

そか

In writing Millie's story, I have had to decide how to present her character. Millie doesn't talk about her feelings, and she is not naturally given to introspection. Though she's absolutely fluent in English, her cadences and inflections owe a lot to a kind of Anglicized Yiddish—"you shouldn't know from this"; "too much I worried about these things." Although I thought at first to restrict myself to her words only, I soon realized that, more than replicating the kind and range of sentences she speaks, my goal had to be to express what I believed was in Millie's heart, even when Millie herself didn't have the words to formulate or express it.

So I wrote what I intuited to be true of Millie's inner world—the desires and fears and hopes and judgments of a young woman, barely more than a girl. And then I read every word to her, every sentence, every revision. Sometimes I wrote things that made her uncomfortable, and we had to negotiate to decide what to keep in and what to take out. (Millie doesn't like talking about herself as being attractive, for example, or having been attractive to men, though I can easily see how she was—and is—and the love scenes with Heniek still make her a little uneasy.) But every sentence that's written here is true to her; every sentence, though it may not so much sound like her, nonetheless to her mind bespeaks her heart, her truth, the reality she lives. "Yes," she says, "it is true; what you have written is true."

As for the historicity of what's written—I can say that everything that can be checked has been checked. The names of the factories in Radom, the names of the various people in charge of the ghettos and the factory where she worked and subsequently of the concentration camp where the laborers lived, the dates of the ghettos' establishment and subsequent liquidations, the death marches. Millie visited Auschwitz in 1987 and brought back a copy of a document that lists the names, birth dates, and occupations of all the arrivals on a certain day during the summer of 1944. Millie is listed, along with her aunt—both from Radom, Millie a "student," her aunt Gittel a "seamstress." And Millie, of course, has a tattoo—A-24542.

The rest is true to Millie's awareness and memory. She was often unsure of sequence and time frame, especially about the tumultuous winter of 1943–1944. She really has no clear sense of how long she was married to Heniek, perhaps months, though sometimes she says it was just a matter of weeks. I've tried to convey this uncertainty in the text, not pretending, after sixty-five years, that she has a full and clear purchase on the exact chronology of specific events. Millie has been determined to be as honest here as she can—about the depth of her love, about the persistence of her hate; about what she remembers and what she doesn't; about what she has clear-cut evidence for and what she can only surmise. She knows she has no access to the causes of things—why the Germans proposed the exchange of Jews for Argentinean citizens, why there was an option of getting on a death wagon on the march to Tomaszów Mazowiecki, whether the way the Radomers put together the sequence of events leading to the death of the thirteen policemen and their families from the factory is really accurate. Millie knows that the story as she tells it is how she and other Radomers in the factory understood what happened. But however strong her accusations, she recognizes that she can't know with complete certainty what in fact did happen.

༄༅

Though Millie can at times be fierce in her judgments, she herself fears the judgments of others even more. She dresses beautifully but simply, often preferring costume jewelry to gems, for example, because she doesn't want people to think her self-indulgent or, worse, that she's trying to call attention to herself. Once, despite her desire, she decided not to go to Israel for a wedding, because she had just been there a couple of weeks earlier for a long-planned visit, and she worried that people might think her extravagant, traveling such a long distance twice within a month. A gentleman friend asked her to dinner, an innocent gesture of companionship between adults who had known each other for more than a half-century, but Millie declined, concerned that others might think it unseemly for her, a widow, to dine with another man.

These are trifles, as she knows. But the fear runs deep, perhaps because exposure to judgment during the war was literally a matter of life or death. Millie never told her sons about her first husband, in large measure because she feared their judgment. She did speak about her experiences to some extent to her family, of course, and sometimes, too, in public, giving talks at synagogues and local Holocaust museums, speaking to schoolchildren, once even traveling to Germany to speak at a high school in Gütersloh, near to where she was interned toward the end of the war in a forced-labor factory. But she never spoke fully or deeply about her past, and she revealed episodes of her life only piecemeal.

This was true to some extent even with Jack. For sixty years, Millie shared her stories with Jack, who, having suffered his own experience of the war, understood whatever she said but was willing not to push when she didn't want to say more. Jack knew that she was briefly married to Heniek and that he was killed, just as Millie knew about Jack's first wife, Rachel, and their three-year-old daughter, Emma, both of whom were also killed. But they respected each other with silence, too, and never pressed the other for details.

Millie resisted telling her sons for a simpler reason—she feared their disdain. What would her children think of her if they knew about Heniek—that she was so young and so much in love; that she was caught in calamity and yet found, though only for a moment, a respite of tenderness and peace. She worried (wrongly) that they would think it improper.

But then it was fear of judgment of another kind that finally prompted her to relent. What if she died and her children never knew why she had kept silent all these years?

Might they suspect her of some wrongdoing? Might they think that she refused to speak because she had something shameful to hide? Though she knows her sons have never given her cause to worry about their judgment of her, she's been much affected by second-generation survivors whose books, to her mind, unfairly critique their parents' lives. Millie doesn't want others to wonder about her story; she wants to claim it for herself.

For sixty-five years, Millie has borne a secret, but she wants it known that her secret is both precious to her and pure. It was then; it is now.

1

He was holding a ring, twirling it between his fingers. It wasn't much of a ring—a thin gold band flecked with a few diamond chips—but he was playing with it, and playing with me, saying, "Whose ring is this? Whose finger will it fit?"

༺ঔৣ༻

It was early autumn, 1945. Jack and I were in Garmisch-Partenkirchen, a small mountain town in southern Germany. I had gone there with my aunt Gittel—I called her Mima—several months after our liberation because we had heard that Radomers were there. Radom, the city we're from in Poland, had factories, like the Steyr-Daimler-Puch factory I worked in, and that meant that Radom had survivors—or at least a greater number of survivors than many other cities—because the Germans had needed workers to help make their war. Hundreds of Radomers had made guns and bullets—the armaments of our own destruction.

Mima and I had spent the first few months after our liberation in Kaunitz, a little town down the road from where we had been freed, but when we heard that other Radomers were in Garmisch-Partenkirchen, we decided to travel the seven hundred kilometers to search for our families. I was looking for my father, and Mima was looking for her husband and son; we had last seen them about a year before, when the men and women were separated at Auschwitz. We decided to go to Garmisch-Partenkirchen even though we didn't really trust the information about the Radomers, because we had also heard that Jack Werber was there, and this we couldn't believe, because everyone from Radom knew that Jack Werber was dead.

Jack was twenty-five in 1939 when the Germans invaded Poland. Suspected of leftist leanings, he was arrested soon afterward and sent to Buchenwald on trumped-up charges of having held communist meetings in the back room of his family's store. I was only twelve when he was arrested and didn't know him, but my family knew his, and we all heard what had happened. Several months after Jack was taken away, his father was called to the offices of the Radom Judenrat and was told that Jack had died of dysentery. If he wanted, Jack's father was told, he could pay to have Jack's ashes sent back to Radom. Devastated that his son had died, Jack's father desperately wanted the ashes. He wanted to give his youngest son a proper burial in the city where his family had lived for a hundred years. So he paid, and several weeks later, a box arrived containing ashes marked as Jack Werber's.

We were so innocent then, so unready to understand what was happening. Jack's was a horrible but plausible story: He had been arrested, had been made to work at a hard labor camp, had gotten sick and died; Jack's captors had cremated his body, and out of some sense of human decency, they had offered to send his ashes home. A sane world, in wartime, might produce such a story. It made sense; it was a story his family was ready to accept.

Except Jack hadn't died. The Germans had simply found a way to extract money from unsuspecting Jews: All over Poland, Jews were told that their sons and fathers and husbands were dead and that they could have the ashes of their family members sent to them for a fee. Jack's father had buried some ashes, but not those of his son.

Had he buried someone else's child? Had he been sent the mixed remains of several people? Perhaps the ashes weren't even a person's. Perhaps Jack's father had buried a dog.

কিত

When Mima and I arrived in Garmisch-Partenkirchen, we found Jack living in an apartment with his cousin Itamar. Itamar, too, had survived the camps. He had set up a little boardinghouse in an apartment building in the center of town. There were about fifteen people in the place, all from Radom— mostly men, plus two of Jack's cousins, Zysla, who was eighteen, like me, and Renya, who was about ten years older.

Mima was ready to move on almost as soon as we arrived, wanting to search for her husband and son and for my father, who we had heard had all gone to Bari, Italy, the port for boats smuggling Jews to Palestine. I wanted to go, too, but Mima thought it better for me to stay in Garmisch-Partenkirchen. I wasn't happy about this, being left behind with people who were pretty much strangers to me, but Mima assured me that Jack would look after me. Jack Werber had a good name, she said; I would be safe with Jack.

I didn't have much of a choice. I did as I was told; I stayed behind.

After Mima left, Zysla and I moved out of Itamar's building to an apartment of our own. It seemed awkward for two young women to be living together with so many men. And I wanted to pay my own way, as it were, to not feel that I was relying on the group for my support. It mattered to me that I not owe anyone anything, that I not be in a position of being asked for something I might be unwilling to give.

So Zysla and I set up in a little apartment down the street, and we came by to Itamar's apartment every morning. We had all been given food stamps, and these entitled us to a certain amount of bread every week. It wasn't enough, but everyone seemed to have a way to get a little extra here and there. One man from Itamar's group, Srulik Rosensweig, worked at the kitchen for the American army, and every few days, he would bring us some cans of soup. Zysla and I used these rations to make breakfast for everyone in the apartment. In the mornings, we would open the cans and skim from the top the little bits of fat floating on the surface. Then we'd spread the slick morsels on the bread we were able to buy with our food stamps. A carbon copy—an *odbitke*—that's what we called it: We'd press two pieces together, the fat would blend from one side to the other, and we'd have carbon copies of bread flavored with

Garmisch-Partenkirchen, 1945. Jack is in the back row,
third from the left; I am third from the right

fat. It was delicious, we thought, this breakfast. And it was
exquisite to be able to eat, to have something to chew, in the
mornings.

In those days, everyone was looking to start over. The young
men wanted to settle down, take care of someone, and have
someone take care of them. They wanted other things, too, of
course, but it was marriage most of all that they were looking
for. If you had a two-minute conversation with a man, he was
ready to make a proposal. Even back in Kaunitz, a young man I
hardly knew—we had taken an evening stroll together once or
twice—gave me a letter offering me "a piece of [his] heart."

Maybe he wanted to marry me—I don't know; I had no interest in that. But all around me, there was matchmaking going on: "How about this one? Do you like her?" "What about so-and-so? He's interested in you." People were trying to inch forward into life.

Once we settled in with the group of Radomers, it seemed there were quite a few men interested in me. I find it embarrassing to say this, mortifying even to admit it at this point in my life. Somehow it feels unseemly to speak of myself in this way, as desirable to men. I prefer to say it more discreetly: I was always lucky with people. And that's true, I was. But it's also true that there were men who wanted me, or wanted to make a match with me. I was fairly young, and there were many more men around than women, and, well, that's the way it was. One man tried to get Jack to speak to me on his behalf—Jack joked to me later that this was like asking the cat to give his milk to the mouse. Another man from our group sometimes would come up behind me, if I was standing at the sink washing dishes or maybe tidying up around the apartment. And then he would start to sing softly to me, just by my ear, so only I could hear. He must have thought his singing was a kind of courtship, that he could woo me with his voice. But I wasn't interested in his attentions, or in anyone's. I had been married once already; I knew I wouldn't marry again.

It was different, though, with Jack. He and I were "just friends," as the young people say today. I was fascinated by him, by his stories, and by the simple fact that he was alive.

A woman among the Radomers—Fela Gutman—advised me to stay away from Jack. She claimed that Jack was sickly, even before the war. His mother had died from tuberculosis when he was only seven years old, and except for his brother

Mannes, who had moved to America before Jack was even born, all of Jack's brothers and sisters were dead. Reared in a house that people thought was tainted by disease, growing up without a mother, eventually the only living member of his immediate family in Europe, and then made to endure five and a half years in Buchenwald—Jack was surely fragile, Fela claimed, somewhat worn out, somewhat spent.

Later I learned that Fela was speaking on behalf of the man who would sing to me—that he had asked her to try to dissuade me from spending time with Jack. But I wasn't convinced by Fela's warnings. I was intrigued more than put off by Jack's history of hardship. What kind of man could have endured what he did? What kind of man could have survived all that? Of the thirty-two hundred Jews and Poles who were taken to Buchenwald with him, only eleven made it to the end of the war. I thought there had to be some kind of strength, something unbreakable inside him, that made it possible for Jack to have survived.

So Jack and I would spend some time together every day—sometimes a walk in the park if the weather was pleasant, sometimes just moments together on the old velvet couch in the apartment's sitting room. Jack would tell me his stories about the war, reluctantly at first and only in response to my pressing him to go on. But eventually his talking eased, encouraged by my interest, and I would listen to him speak, filled with admiration and pity, in equal measure.

For the first fourteen weeks that he was interned in Buchenwald, Jack was made to work in the rock quarry. Twelve hours a day in the frigid German winter, Jack hoisted boulders onto his shoulders and then carried them up the 150 steps to the upper rim of the quarry, where he would dump his load onto a rock pile. He wore only the single thin layer of his ragged uniform and on his feet cumbersome wooden clogs, whose hard, unbending bottoms made it nearly impossible for him to walk steadily over the uneven ground. I knew these clogs; I too suffered from them in Auschwitz: They became, literally for me, the stuff of nightmares. The punishment for falling down in the quarry or for resting from one's labors was either a beating or immediate execution. As far as Jack knew at the time, there was no purpose to this work, only the intent, precisely, to break the backs of the prisoners. He told me that dozens of men died every day in this detail, either from physical exhaustion or from getting shot by one of the fifty soldiers standing guard. One day, he told me, three hundred men left the barracks for work in the morning and only two hundred returned at night.

Jack claimed not to know how he managed to survive his fourteen weeks in the quarry—or his five and a half years in Buchenwald—but as I listened to his stories in the weeks after we met, I came to see how he managed.

In the quarry, for example, every time Jack reached the bottom of the pit, he told me, he would make a quick inspection of the stones before choosing one to lift, trying to determine which ones might look heavier than they really were. He couldn't actually test them out, by shoving them around with his foot, say, to feel their weight, because that would risk his getting noticed by a guard. He had to figure this out by sight— maybe one stone had an indentation on the bottom, maybe another was shaped in a way that made the weight easier to distribute across his shoulders. He observed, he experimented, and over the days and weeks, he learned which stones were the best to lift.

One time, he got caught.

Jack was working in a building detail that involved carrying materials—bags of cement, heavy stones, and such—to and from a construction site. He and a partner carried their loads by holding on to the ends of two horizontal poles attached to the sides of a large wooden box in which the materials would be stacked. They bore all the weight of the box in their uncovered hands: blisters formed, then opened, and still they had to carry the box with its load bearing down on their raw and oozing palms. Jack devised a contraption to ease the pain: Scavenging among some discarded building materials, he found a bit of rope, drew it up one sleeve, across his shoulders and down his other arm; then he tied the ends of the rope to the poles. When the stinging in his hands got too much to bear, Jack would loosen his grip and let the rope across his shoulders carry the weight. An ingenious device—simple and effective and secret.

Until it was not so secret. A guard spotted the rope and charged him with sabotage for stealing the property of the Third Reich. The rope was garbage, but that was apparently irrelevant. Jack was taken to a tree, his hands tied behind his back, the rope tying them together tied in turn to an outstretched limb, and he was left to hang there, along with two other "saboteurs," dangling backward, his shoulders slowly being pulled from their sockets.

Jack. Dear Jack. What he was made to suffer. Whatever I had been through, I had not been through anything like this. I could feel my heart softening to him, his cleverness, his uncompromising virtue.

An SS officer accused a man Jack was working with of being lazy and, on a whim, set as a punishment that Jack should bury the man alive in a deep hole near the place they were working. When Jack hesitated, the officer told the other man to bury Jack instead. Fearful, Jack supposed, of what punishment might result from his refusal to follow the command, Jack's partner obeyed the order. He pushed Jack into the hole and began to shovel in the dirt heaped up in a mound nearby, with the officer calmly watching. As the dirt piled up, past Jack's waist and then up to his chest, Jack started to take very deep breaths, expanding his lungs to their capacity each time, hoping to create some space to breathe. Jack's fellow prisoner kept shoveling, stopping every few minutes to stomp the dirt down with his feet. He had been given a job to do, and he was trying, Jack supposed, to do it well. When the dirt reached Jack's neck, the officer, perhaps suddenly changing his mind or perhaps just tiring of the spectacle, told the prisoner to dig out all the dirt and release Jack from the hole. He scolded Jack for being unwilling to bury the man who was so quickly willing to bury him. Then the officer beat the other prisoner with his baton and walked away.

It was a lucky escape. The officer could just as easily have chosen to let Jack be buried alive as release him.

כ״ה

This story—and the many others like it—drew me to Jack. He seemed truly heroic to me, a real hero of a man, and not only because of the obvious—in 1944, he had helped save seven hundred boys who had come to Buchenwald destined for death—but because of this determination to be a *mensch* in the world, no matter what the context, no matter what the result. I was proud to know him; I was proud, truly, to be associated with him among all the Radomers in our group. And I found myself wanting to make him happy, to try somehow to make up for all the miseries he had been made to suffer.

But I wanted nothing more—nothing more than the stories and the quiet time in conversation. So when we were sitting together one day, and Jack took that ring from his pocket, rolling it around between his fingers, I didn't respond when he asked me whom it might fit. I knew what he meant. But I couldn't answer his question. Maybe I just smiled a little and bent my head away.

You see, liberation for me didn't feel like a new beginning. You watch these old-time newsreels now of towns across Europe being liberated by the Allied troops, and everyone is out on the streets looking happy and relieved, and women are throwing themselves at the soldiers and hugging and kissing them. As if liberation were the end of it all. As if liberation meant a fresh start. As if it meant real, uncluttered freedom. But that's not how it was—not for me. I had been "liberated," yes. But into what? Liberated into an abyss, an oblivion, into a life without moorings.

My brother, Majer, had been shot to death by German soldiers during the liquidation of the Radom ghetto in the summer of 1942. Mima had watched it happen. She told me, too, that my mother and grandparents had been taken away at the same time—to Treblinka, as we later learned. My father and

My brother, Majer Drezner, circa 1927

uncle had escaped the deportations because they, like my aunt and me, had managed to find work, but Mima and I hadn't seen the men since our arrival at Auschwitz. And Heniek, my husband, was dead. That I knew. That I could feel as a certainty in my blood.

At the moment of my liberation, two thoughts came upon me, very clear and very precise. The first was laced with bitterness, and I spit it out like some bad taste that had lingered in my mouth for years: "I don't want to be Jewish anymore; it's a death sentence to be Jewish." The other thought rose in me more forcibly from my gut, like a tight knot at the bottom of my belly, a query rather than a claim: "To whom do I belong, and who belongs to me?"

That question had sounded in my head every day since my liberation. I enjoyed being with Jack; I felt comfortable with him. But I refused to let myself fall in love, and I knew I would never marry again. There had already been too much love in my life, and too much loss. I couldn't risk another loss. And I wouldn't betray my first love. To be true, I couldn't fall in love with Jack because I was still so deeply in love with Heniek.

I must explain this love, I know. I was barely more than a child, just fifteen when I first fell in love. The world was falling to pieces, and I was lost and frightened and on my own. I loved a man twelve years my senior, and at sixteen I married him with joy in my heart. In some way, and secretly, I have loved him ever since.

To tell this story, I have to go back, closer to the beginning. I have to go back to the ghetto.

2

MY MOTHER WAS ALWAYS WORKING. THIS IS MY CLEAREST memory of her—Mama at the sewing table, cutting fabric freehand, without patterns, sewing pieces together, making miracles out of bits of cloth. I am a young girl watching her, and I am amazed by the magic of it—that she somehow knows where to cut, where to stitch, as if the material has some kind of inner logic that she is able to follow without the bother of paper patterns. The swoosh of the dark material as it glides and comes to rest on the table where she works; the dust of the marking chalk floating in the air; the girls who work for her gathered together in focused concentration. It is a mystery to me and a wonder, how Mama can turn these flat and lifeless waves of cloth into the clothes her customers so desire. And how beautiful the clothing is! The dresses and blouses and skirts, all understated but somehow elegant, too. The ladies from the town arrive, Jews, of course, but Gentiles, as well, wearing their fur-trimmed coats and carrying leather

Radom postcard, 1930s

handbags. They love my mother's clothes. I know they give her money for her work, but sometimes I see they give her bread instead. One time, maybe this is early in 1941—I am not yet fourteen years old, we have just moved to the ghetto, and there are still a few Polish customers who come to see my mother—a woman arrives carrying a thick book in her gloved hand. I know this woman; she has been coming for years. She is a bit formal perhaps, but kind as well, friendly even to me, as I watch the goings-on from the back of the room, trying not to get in the way. The woman lays her book down on the table to remove her gloves and set down her purse. I look over to see the title: *Mein Kampf*.

⟨ᴑ⟩

Mama and I shared a bed. Before we moved to the ghetto, we lived in a large, two-room apartment in the center of Radom near City Hall, on Wolnosc Street. The second of the two rooms was separated across the middle by two large wooden wardrobe cabinets in which Mama kept her sewing materials. In the back section of the room were two beds, one for my father and brother and one for Mama and me. My father lived in Paris for the first seven years of my life— I think he felt it would be easier to make a living there than in Poland—but even when he came home in 1935, he slept with my brother, and Mama with me. I loved being in bed with Mama, nestling in her warmth at night under the feather blanket.

In Europe in those days, it wasn't the way it is now in America, where parents endlessly praise their children and

Majer, Mama, and me

hug and kiss them every day. Mama didn't hug me much, and I don't remember her ever telling me that she loved me. "Why do I have to tell my daughter I love her?" she would have wondered. "Of course I love her; I'm her mother!" I didn't miss it, though, because I didn't know anything else. Besides, in bed, I didn't need Mama's words; I felt her love every night in her bone-weary embrace. Sometimes I would massage her feet before she fell off to sleep, her muscles slowly releasing, softly relaxing in my hands. Then I would crawl under the feather blanket with her and feel her warm breath on my back.

The front part of the large room served as both living room and salon for Mama's customers. She laid out ladies' magazines on a little coffee table she set there, and her clients would flip through the pages and choose the items they wanted her to make.

The kitchen was the workroom, with a large table in the center, where my mother stood for hours cutting and sewing her fabrics. She taught me to cut the fabric exactly right, because material was expensive and her clients always wanted to buy just a bit less than they really needed. If Mama told them they needed three yards to make a dress, they'd buy two and a half yards instead to save a little money. So there was no room for error; every cut had to count.

At the height of her business before the war began, Mama had four women sewing for her. They worked long hours, but

Mama is second from the right; Mima is sitting beside her

she treated them well and helped them save up to buy sewing machines for themselves. That was a big deal, a sewing machine. It was transportable, first of all, so no matter where you had to go, no matter what the situation, you could take the machine with you and earn a living. When the ghetto was established in 1941 and we had to leave our apartment on Wolnosc Street and move in with Mima and my uncle and their two children, Mama brought along her sewing machine. She had hoped that she could continue to work, even in the ghetto. But there was no room to sew—eight of us at that point were living in a single room—and after the first month or two in the ghetto, there were no customers. One of the girls who worked for Mama managed to leave Poland before the war began. She went to Paris, and she brought her machine with her so she could work, so she could live.

Mama wanted me to learn to sew so that I would have a trade. Sewing and embroidery were the two professions acceptable for girls. Mama was successful in her business—she kept us housed and fed—but it seemed to me that she worked all the time, until we lit candles on Friday night and then again as soon as Shabbos was over. When my father lived away, it was Mama who supported me and my brother. My father did send home some money, I think, and I know he sent occasional treats—canned sliced pineapple, for example, which I happily devoured between pieces of buttered cornbread—but it was my mother's sewing business that kept our household together. I was young—barely a teenager—and Mama wanted to teach me, too. Perhaps she had a sense that a woman needed to learn to provide for herself, in case she had no one else to rely on.

I once saw her reading a letter from my father. Sitting on our bed in the back of our apartment with the unfolded paper in

Mima and Feter, 1932

her hands, she quietly, quietly cried. I hated that; I hated to see those tears. And I hated, too, to see how hard she had to work with my father away. I knew I didn't want that for myself, to work all day at the cutting table, to spend every day with scissors and needles and thread.

I didn't want to work, but work is what saved me in the war.

སྐྱ

In the spring of 1941, when we moved to the ghetto, Mama took her sewing machine and one of the two beds from the back room of our apartment; she also took the feather blankets. Everything else we owned—the furniture, the dishes, the cutlery—we had to leave behind. Mima and my uncle—I called him Feter—had found a single-room apartment on

Szwarlikowska Street, in the area of the city that the Germans closed off to make the ghetto, and we moved in with them. We had three beds for the eight of us: Mima and Feter and their two children shared two beds, I still got to sleep with Mama, and my father and brother slept on the floor. We had no bathroom—there was an outhouse in the back—and no running water. The wooden floor was painted white; in the winter, the cold made the boards seize up and creak in the night.

I was frightened of the ghetto, even from the start.

I had never really known hunger before; we weren't rich among the Jews of Radom, but we had what we needed—a meal every day with potatoes and meat, on Friday nights a chicken. In the ghetto, I began to learn what hunger is.

We got ration cards, some kind of food stamps, and we had to stand in line for hours at one of the few bakeries still working for our small ration of bread. Sometimes, when we finally got our turn at the bakery window, we would be told that there was no more bread to be had, that they had already run out. So Mama suggested that we all go to different places to increase our chances. Mama sometimes sent me to stay with a cousin of ours who lived in a building whose ground floor housed one of the bakeries. I would sleep on our cousin's floor for a few hours at night and then get up at three o'clock in the morning. It would still be dark, of course, and bitter cold, but if I got to the courtyard before there was even a hint of morning in the air, I had a chance of returning home with warm bread in my hands. On those occasions, I was triumphant: "Look, Mama, look what I have brought. A loaf of bread!" A treasure.

I didn't like to be on the streets. I didn't really like to be any-where outside our single room. Even before the ghetto, before the war, I was frightened of Poles. Jews were never accepted by them; we never felt a part of their society. Jews weren't allowed to work in any official or government-related jobs—not in banks or on the trains or in the post office. Growing up, I knew to stay away from the Poles, the boys especially, who sometimes threw stones at us. If we saw Polish people walking down the street, we always crossed to the other side. If we ever saw a priest—I don't know why we did this—we would always hold on to a shirt or coat button. There was somehow supposed to be protection in that small gesture. No priest ever accosted me or anyone I knew, but I knew I was supposed to be wary of priests, to stay away, to clutch a button.

In the ghetto, the danger was real and routine. Once, com-ing home from the bakery in the early morning, I passed Chavela Mora, a cousin of mine, on the street. We were the same age and had lived in the same building before the ghetto was established. I used to envy her beauty, with her big brown eyes and a full head of luxuriant blonde curls; my hair was al-ways fine and thin. But now I saw that she was utterly changed. She looked maybe half her former size; she was sprawled out on the sidewalk, her arm outstretched, begging for coins, and all her hair had fallen out. She clearly hadn't eaten—or washed—in a very long time. Perhaps she had typhus. She looked desper-ately alone and bewildered, out on the street, with people passing by. What happened to her parents? Why weren't they there, taking care of her?

It's hard to consider a question like this. It's hard for a fourteen-year-old girl even to formulate such a question.

I called out to my cousin, but her gaze didn't move to meet mine. I was frightened, too frightened to approach her, though I wanted to and thought perhaps I should. I ran home and told Mama what I had seen, but no one could find Chavela after that.

Maybe she had been taken away.

They did that, in the ghetto. The Germans would take people randomly off the streets, and no one would ever see them again. People would go out in the day, maybe to try to sell something or find some food, and they would never return. This has to be a child's greatest fear. Certainly it was mine. To be snatched away and never found.

This is what happened to Motel Rafalowitz. Or something close to this, anyway.

Motel had left his apartment early one morning to get his family's ration of bread. Hours passed and then several days, but Motel never came home. Somehow Motel's wife, Dina Rosa, eventually learned that Motel was in the Radom jail, having been arrested when he went looking for bread on the Aryan side of town, outside the ghetto. Then we heard—though I have no idea how this information got around—that Motel was going to be executed and that he was going to have to pass by the ghetto wall on his way. Everyone scrambled to see him. Dina Rosa, of course, but many others, too. I went with Mama; I think my brother came, as well. I remember several young boys trying to climb the brick wall that separated the ghetto from the outside world to reach their heads over the top to see.

We waited for a long while, Dina Rosa screaming out her husband's name at intervals. And then we heard him—the boys on the wall said Motel was being held between two soldiers. They were passing by just on the other side.

"Motel!" Dina Rosa called out. "Motel, I am here!"

"Dina Rosa!" he cried as he passed. "Dina Rosa! Throw me a piece of bread. They're going to shoot me!"

Even then I understood the anguish of that cry. In his last moments, more than his wife, more than escape, Motel's deepest desire was simply for bread, a bite of bread before the gun fired.

Dina Rosa collapsed against the ghetto wall, sobbing as Mama took her in her arms. Mama was swaying back and forth with Dina Rosa's heaving cry, trying to comfort the poor woman. But I wanted comfort, too. I wanted those arms about me, Mama clutching me to her breast.

It wasn't a scene for a child, for a young girl to see. Motel starving and all alone, with no one able to rescue him. Dina Rosa, disbelieving and empty, for whom all rescue was impossible.

I was fourteen, and I was scared.

❧

I was thinking of Jedlińsk.

It's 1940, the year before the ghetto was established, and we're still living on Wolnosc Street. I'm thirteen years old. My father has left Radom for Jedlińsk, a small village about fifteen kilometers outside of town. We have relatives there, I know, but it's not entirely clear to me why he has taken off. My uncle has left Radom, too. He is a member of a socialist Zionist group, the Left Po'alei Zion, and he has gone to Russia to see if he can arrange safe passage for Mima and their children.

Mama tells me something vague about why my father has left home, but I don't understand entirely what she's saying. It has something to do with their fearing his arrest, but I don't see why anyone would want to arrest my father. Perhaps I don't know him that well—I have never managed to feel close to him since he returned from his many years away in Paris—but I do know that he isn't a criminal in any way.

After a few days, Mama tells me I have to go to him, to give him a message from her that he should stay in Jedlińsk for another week. There is going to be another *oblava*, another roundup of Jews in Radom—I don't know how she knows this—and he should stay away. My brother, Majer, cannot go—he is sixteen now, and he will surely be recognized as a Jew. It is also impossible for my mother to go. She too will easily be recognized, and how would we manage without her? So I must go. I am thirteen, and I must go on my own to Jedlińsk to tell my father not to return to Radom.

I am scared. Mama! This is against the law, what you are asking me to do. If I get caught, Mama! What will happen if I get caught?

Mama dresses me as a peasant girl: She puts a babushka on my head and tells me to take off my shoes. Peasants walk barefoot. I do as I am told. I wear my old coat, but Mama removes from my sleeve the white armband with the blue Magen David that I must wear as a Jew. This is the greatest crime—for a Jew to walk in the street without the armband bearing the Star of David. But Mama takes mine off and takes my face between her hands; she kisses my forehead.

"You must go now, Maniusia." She uses a diminutive of my name, an endearment. "You must go tell your father to stay in Jedlińsk."

So I walk, barefoot and trembling, out of Radom and onto the lanes leading to the village fifteen kilometers away. My feet begin to hurt as soon as the city streets give way to country roads—I am not accustomed to walking without shoes, and the twigs and pebbles scattered across the lanes dig into my soles. I keep my head down, scared to catch anyone's eye, scared to be asked what I am doing, a Jew in unconvincing costume.

Eventually, an old man comes by driving a horse and wagon and offers me a ride toward the village. I accept, grateful to get off my feet. I don't remember much else—how, after the man dropped me off still some distance from the village, I managed to find my cousins' house, how long I stayed there, or what I may have said to my father. It's all a blankness to me, a darkness I can't penetrate. I have no idea now how I returned home.

What stays with me is my fear, rising up with the sting of bile in my gut as I walked along. Mama, who had cradled me in her arms every night of my life, had sent me out to walk alone, exposed on country lanes. Mama had sent me into danger.

At times in the night, somewhere deep down, I still feel the fear of that thirteen-year-old girl, a vague foreboding about what comes next. That feeling has nestled inside me; it can lie dormant for long stretches of time, but it has never gone away.

♦

The Germans never came looking for my father, as far as I know. They did come for my uncle, though. It was the next year, and they went rampaging through the ghetto, banging on people's doors, arresting those with socialist affiliations.

The Germans had already conducted oblavas for other groups. The intelligentsia, the doctors, and the butchers and water carriers, too, maybe because, either through education or brute strength, these men could be trouble if they organized resistance groups. But on this day, the Germans came looking for the leftists, and the soldiers came into our building looking particularly for my uncle, my Feter, Yisroel Glatt.

"Glatt! Where is Yisroel Glatt?" they screamed, angry already.

They had lists of names. I suppose their informers had told them things—who belonged to which organization, who perhaps was trying to stash what where. They burst into our building, clutching their lists, pounding through the hallways

Feter, center, and friends

with their heavy boots, calling out the names of those they were looking for.

They banged on our door.

"Glatt. We're here for Yisroel Glatt."

I knew what they could do. I knew what these soldiers were capable of. Even on a whim, even just for fun.

Some time before, early on in the war, perhaps in September or October 1939, the soldiers had come for Majer Berger, a Torah scribe who lived in our building. He was a quiet man with gentle eyes that creased at the corners when he smiled at me and a light red beard stained murky yellow in places—from cigarettes, I suppose, though I never saw him smoke. He had four small boys; I guess he was in his forties, but I was just twelve at the time, and he seemed ancient to me, the very essence of a religious man. I'm sure he was pious; I probably thought he was close to sacred.

When the Germans came for him, he offered no resistance. I didn't even know until late in the day that he had been taken. When he returned later in the evening, I saw him in the hallway. He walked slowly, pressing his hand against the wall for support. A good part of his beard was gone and his face was smeared with blood. Mama pulled me into the apartment, wanting to shield me from such sights. The next day, I learned the story from others in the building: The Germans had taken Mr. Berger and two other bearded Jews down to the Jewish high school at 27 Żeromskiego Street. They lined up the men by a tree and then, one by one, grabbed bits of their beards and yanked the hairs out from their bleeding chins. Just like that, the soldiers pulled out the beards of these harmless men. Then the men were made to climb the tree and balance themselves on the branches. The soldiers ordered them to yell out "cuckoo" to each other, obedient show-birds put on display. The Germans were suitably entertained, gawking at the men, laughing and joking as Mr. Berger and the two others tried not to fall. After a time, the men were permitted to come down from the tree and return to their homes.

How is a young girl to understand the meaning of an event like this? A child understands schoolyard meanness, classroom mischief. Jack once told me that when he was a boy and was made to study with some very old and, he said, very smelly rabbi

Me, circa 1935

who had a tendency to nod off during their lessons, he and some of the other boys in the class would sometimes glue little bits of the rabbi's beard to the study table as he slept. The boys would get a laugh—and a good hard smack—when the rabbi awoke. Little Jewish boys, studying Talmud, playing at pranks.

But this—what happened with Mr. Berger—was something else. There was blood and, in Mr. Berger's eyes, a confused look that I didn't understand—bewilderment and fear and defeat all at once. I stared, a young girl in braided pigtails, cowering in my mother's arms.

When they came for my uncle, I thought of Motel Rafalowitz and old Majer Berger, and again I was scared.

The Germans didn't find Feter that day—he was still in Russia at that point and returned only a few months later after he realized he wouldn't be able to arrange for his family's transport. But not finding my uncle just seemed to anger the soldiers more. They stormed down the hall and banged on the door of another family. Here, too, lived a man named Glatt, but not my uncle, not any relation of his, and not, as far as any of us knew, involved in the Left Po'alei Zion or any other socialist group. Nonetheless, his name was Glatt. The Germans had Glatt on their list, and they were determined to get a Glatt.

This Glatt they found, and they grabbed him out of his apartment, his family screaming, "Please, please, don't take him," Glatt himself trying to tell them they had the wrong man. It was useless to plead; it was useless to cry.

They shot him in the hall.

I remained with Mama in our room, trying not to hear.

אמ

When the German army put up a flyer in the ghetto announcing that Jews aged fifteen to forty could register for work at the Steyr-Daimler-Puch factory just outside of town, I didn't want to go. It was the summer of 1942, and although the ghetto was dreadful to me, I barely ever wanted to venture out of the cramped room we shared. I was determined never to leave my family. Everything seemed so precarious in the ghetto. I didn't trust that anything would stay in place if I didn't watch it all the time. If I went away to work and live at the factory, what would be left when I returned?

I didn't want to go.

It was my uncle, my Feter, who made me. He had returned from Russia by this time and was adamant that all of us try to find work. "If you work," he said, "you might live."

My brother had been chosen for work as a street sweeper. Majer had already studied at a private Jewish high school, which was a big honor in those days; if you could graduate from high school and get your *matura*—that was considered the mark of a truly educated man. But in the ghetto, work of any kind was precious, and he had been relieved to have a job. One day, though, as he was sweeping the street, he was knocked over by German soldiers driving by in a truck. They were laughing, he told me, pleased that they had run down a Jew. He broke his leg in the fall. Mama tried to set it straight, but he walked with a limp after that.

When the factory announced that they would take Jewish workers, Majer couldn't go—they wouldn't take anyone they considered disabled. My father and aunt and uncle had already managed to get jobs: My father worked in the Kromolowski factory, where they made saddles, Feter worked in a tannery, and Mima was a seamstress in a shop where she made and mended clothes for the Germans. But Mama and I needed work, and even though she was over forty, Mama said she would go with me to the munitions factory to register.

It didn't take long for the Germans to sort through the many people who showed up. I was accepted without question; I was young, thin, and delicate, but in apparent good health. At forty-three, Mama was too old. They wouldn't take her. She was sent back to the ghetto, and I was left at the factory, alone.

I wanted desperately to go with her, to return to the ghetto and stay with her and the rest of our little family. I wanted to be able to sleep beside her, to feel her warmth surround me. Always that, maybe mostly that—the warmth of Mama's ample body in the night. Despite the oblavas, the unprovoked brutalities, the sickness and the hunger and the dread that were upon me, still, I wanted only to be with Mama in the ghetto.

Yet I was not allowed. I was made to stay at the factory. Feter said, and the family agreed, if you work, you might live. So, at fifteen, I began to work in the ammunitions factory, and after that first day at work, I never spent another night with my mother again.

❦

The factory was a large building a couple of kilometers out of town. Poles had worked there previously, but they were paid, whereas we were available as slave labor—unpaid and barely fed—so the Germans brought us in to replace the Poles. We were set to work at enormous machines for twelve-hour shifts, six hours at a time with a fifteen-minute break between. We worked either 6 A.M. to 6 P.M. or 6 P.M. to 6 A.M. I worked at a machine drilling holes into little metal slugs. I was given measurements—the hole had to be so wide and so deep—and it had to be exact. I was required to drill fifteen hundred pieces per shift—one after the other, hour after hour, day after day. No talking, no sitting. Just drilling holes into metal slugs, precisely so wide, precisely so deep, and placing each one as I finished it into compartmentalized wooden boxes at my side. If I worked, I could live. I was grateful for that. But I knew I could not make a mistake. Mistakes would not be tolerated.

This I learned within days of arriving at the factory. There was a young man, Weinberg was his name. He was a friend of my brother's—probably eighteen or so at the time. One day, I saw Weinberg running fast across the grounds, toward the gates of the compound. I wondered why he was sprinting; he, of course, had nowhere to go. Then I saw the soldiers running, too, carrying their rifles, raising them to shoot. And then they did—shoot him, I mean. They raised their rifles and shot this young man dead. Just like that. He crumpled into the dirt, the force of the bullets first propelling him forward, as if pushing him onward for a moment in his desperate stride, but then, and really all at once, because it could have taken only a second or two, Weinberg collapsed on the ground.

Feter! You told me that working would protect me, that if I work I will live. I am here in this factory, I am here drilling these holes. The dreadful noise of these monstrous machines, the metal dust in the air, the monotony of the endless hours, the loneliness, the fear. My legs ache from standing so long.

All so I can live. But what about Weinberg? Weinberg has been working, too, yet he has been killed.

Weinberg, it seemed, had made some kind of mistake; that's what the Germans said. They said he was trying to sabotage the ammunition. When the Germans accused him of this crime, he knew what it meant and so he ran. Then he was shot. Then he fell. Then the Germans dragged his body away.

Alone in the factory, I knew I must not make a mistake.

During the first several weeks that I worked at the factory—while they were building barracks on Skolzna Street for the twenty-five hundred workers who eventually came there—we were housed in a building that seemed something like a horse arena. I don't really know what the building was, what it had been intended for, but after the summer of 1942, it became a place for the women, Jewish slave-laborers, to sleep. It was an empty, cavernous structure with a hard cement floor and, around the perimeter, something that looked like a trough. We used this as our latrine. We slept without bedding, without blankets, on the floor.

After a few weeks—this must have been midsummer—we were told by the factory supervisor, a German named Briticleiber, that we could return to the ghetto for several hours to collect and bring back to the factory anything we thought was valuable. He told us that something was about to happen and that if we wanted to bring things to keep for after the war, the Germans would save them for us. He didn't say so explicitly, but we knew from this little speech that there would be another oblava in the ghetto, perhaps a large one this time.

I walked back to the ghetto. Of course, we didn't have anything of real value—my mother had her sewing machine, but what use would I have for that? We had no diamonds or gold or silver. But I went back because I was told I could go and because I wanted to see my family. I was determined not to return to the factory; I wanted to stay with my family in the ghetto, no matter what.

When I got home, I spoke my mind: "I don't want to go back. I just want to be with all of you. Please. I want to stay."

I was begging. I wanted to be grown-up for my family, to do what they asked of me, but I wanted my mother more, and all I could do was plead.

My uncle insisted. He was adamant, cruel. I can still hear his words, his face red with pain and fury. "No," he said. "Send her out. Throw her out from the house. She must go. She must go to work."

It was beyond comprehension, I thought, to drive a daughter away like that, to send her out on her own when all she wanted was to be home. I was lost, conquered by the clarity of his conviction.

I cried. Mama tried to comfort me. She kissed my cheek.

"You must go, Maniusia. It is for the best."

Mama asked me where I slept, and I told her about the cold cement ground. She handed me our feather blanket to take back.

That was my valuable, Mama's last gift to me, and that was the last time I ever saw her, sending me off on my own, back to the German ammunitions factory. It felt like banishment; it felt like desertion.

The next day, the large-scale deportations began. We knew something big was going to happen, because the Germans set up floodlights in the town, so many lights and so bright that even a couple of kilometers away, as we were, it seemed like daylight in the deepest hours of the night.

The city of Radom was almost entirely liquidated of Jews in two large deportations during August 1942. Before the war started, about thirty thousand Jews lived there, comprising one-third of the total population. The first deportation occurred on August 5, when the Glinice Ghetto was liquidated; that was the smaller of the two ghettos the Germans established in Radom and the one where my family lived. Eleven days later, and over the course of three days, from August 16 to August 18, the large ghetto was cleared out. My brother was killed during this deportation, executed because, with his limp, he was considered unfit for work. My mother was taken away; she had been working in a shop, which should have protected her, but the soldiers came in anyway, and rounded up all the workers to fulfill some quota they had. I learned this later from my uncle. My grandparents and most of my cousins were taken away that day, as well.

In all her life, Mama had never traveled, had never been on a train to anywhere. Like her parents and grandparents, my mother, Dvora Ajchenbaum Drezner, was married and lived all her days in Radom. The first time Mama got on a train was the last time, too: Her first train trip was in the cattle car that took her to Treblinka.

After the deportations, few Jews remained in Radom. For another year or so, until November 1943, the ghetto still stood, populated mostly by Jews who had found work in the stores and workshops the Germans had taken over; some Jews also got sent to the ghetto from the surrounding villages. Mima and Feter stayed for nearly a year longer in their room on Szwarlikowska Street before they, too, came to the factory, in November 1943.

After the deportations, though, I no longer wanted to be in the ghetto. My brother had been killed; my mother, my grand-

Majer, Mama, and me

parents, and most of my aunts and uncles—they had all been taken away. What was left there for me? I didn't understand the grown-ups, why they continued in their pathetic daily routines. Searching for bread, scavenging for wood, finding a mitten, maybe a scarf, to keep warm. Why did the world not end? I didn't understand this. Mama was gone; my brother was dead. Why did life go on?

No one sat *shivah* for my brother or for anyone else. Death was everywhere, yet no one mourned in any way that I could see. This I couldn't bear. Not because of the religious part—not because of some religious obligation to perform a ritual. Even then, this is not what mattered to me. But because it felt as if no one were willing to think about the meaning of things, to make the deaths and the deportations echo in some way. Perhaps I am able to see it differently now: With so much death, how could one sit shivah? One would be sitting shivah continuously for years. But at fifteen, I thought it a meanness of some kind, an intolerable indifference, a crusting-over of the soul, and I was too young for that, despite my surroundings.

After the deportations, I hated to be in the ghetto. I went back a few times—for the ring, for the wedding—but I no longer had, and wouldn't have again for years to come, anything I could think of as home. The ghetto was now to me only a place of loss, of fear, and of death. I preferred the factory, with its numbing routine, with Mama's feather blanket, and, at least for a time, with Heniek.

3

Heniek Greenspan was a policeman.

They were Jews, these policemen, and generally well respected in the community, or at least they had been before the war began. They were men in their prime, able-bodied and agile, and most of them had achieved their *matura* diploma at least. The Germans used them to carry out their policies in the ghetto and the factory. The policemen would designate people for forced-work details, guard the perimeter of the ghetto, and oversee the distribution of our meager food rations. Though they didn't carry guns, they were given certain privileges for their services to the Germans. They could go into and out of the ghetto, for example, without explicit permission, and in the factory, some had separate rooms of their own—they didn't live as the rest did, in crowded barracks. Not all of them, certainly, but most of the Jewish police felt that they had special protection as well as privileges with the Germans, and given the circumstances, the police tended to look upon themselves as better than everyone else.

Nojich Tannenbaum, for example, was this way. He was an informer as well as a policeman, and he would boast to us that his family—his wife, their young twin girls, their Jewish maid, all of them—would survive on an island of safety while everything else around them burned. He patrolled the factory grounds, supervising—spying, really—looking for anything he could report to the Germans. Maybe someone was hiding extra food; maybe someone was not where he or she was supposed to be. No one ever wanted to see Tannenbaum or be seen by him; certainly no one trusted him. He was a Jew, but he was working for the Germans, seemingly with the wholeness of his heart. I was told that Sturmbannführer Wilhelm Blum, the SS officer who planned and carried out the liquidation of the ghettos, was the godfather of his twins.

Tannenbaum didn't know it then—when we were in the factory, none of us did—but the Germans would save no special treatment for their informers and police. In the end, those who had served the Germans would be used and murdered just like the rest of us. Tannenbaum was murdered, though not by the Germans. He was killed by Jews at Auschwitz, exacting their own kind of justice against someone who had caused so much death.

There was Chiel Friedman, too, with whom I had such dealings later on. Chiel Friedman was a friend of Feter's from long before the war. They had known each other for years; Feter and he were members of the same socialist Zionist youth organization. During the war, though, Friedman became a member of the Jewish police, and he became proud, arrogant, cruel.

After the ghetto was liquidated, Feter appealed to Friedman to help find work for my cousin, Moishele, who was only thirteen at the time. He was too young, officially, to work for the Germans, who accepted people for work details only if they were fifteen or older. Feter called out to Friedman one day in the street.

"Chiel," he said, "I need your help." My uncle was calling out to a man who had been a friend, with whom he had once dreamed of a better world, a socialist paradise in which all men would be equal.

Friedman came over to my uncle, looked him in the eye, and slapped him hard across the face.

"I am not Chiel Friedman anymore," he said. "I am Commander Friedman. That is what you must call me." And he turned on his boot and walked away.

Feter told me this story after the war had ended. He wanted to explain that what Friedman had done to me—because by that time, I had cause to despise him, too—was characteristic of this man and not directed at me personally. When the two of them were together in Dachau, Feter told me, Friedman would force the men to stand longer than necessary in their twice-daily *appels*, or roll calls. It could be raining or snowing, the sun could be beating down on them, the winter wind could be whipping through their flimsy uniforms—whatever the weather, it didn't matter. Chiel Friedman made them stand for a half hour, sometimes an hour longer than the Germans required. Friedman seemed to want to prove himself; he wanted to show the Germans, and maybe the Jews, too, that he knew how to be cruel and indiscriminate in his cruelty.

When Dachau was liberated, Feter told me, Friedman approached him to make peace, to shake his hand, as if now there would be a future for them to share together, as if now

Friedman's time as a policeman could be buried. Friedman put his hand out toward my uncle, but Feter refused to take it.

"For me the war has ended," Feter said, "but for you it has just begun."

And this was true. Friedman lived a hellish life after the war. The Radomer survivors spurned him, refusing to offer him the help and community they were so eager to offer to each other. Chiel Friedman lived as an outcast.

This is what it was like to be a policeman in the ghetto, in the factory—to be someone with power when Jews were not allowed to have any power; to be someone who could give and enforce orders and mete out punishments if those orders were not followed; to be someone who had the license to be self-interested at others' expense. The police were danger-ous, and we feared them nearly as much as we feared our German captors.

צבי

Heniek seemed different. He was charming, and in the early days at the factory, even before the barracks were built, he would come into the horse arena to check on the women, not so much to supervise as simply to see if we were okay. I kept mostly to myself—I was on my own in a strange place, without my family, without knowing how I was to manage day to day. I slept beside a girl I knew from Radom, Sally Apel, but I felt separated from all the others there. I was a good deal younger than most of the women, and I was timid. I always spoke softly, almost to myself. I didn't like to look at people directly, for fear that they would look directly back. It has always been in my nature to be somewhat inconspicuous, quiet, in the corners.

The women were all smitten with Heniek—he was slim and tall, with thick, wavy dark hair and the softest brown eyes. Even I could tell that he was handsome. He spoke to the women gently, quietly, even when he came to give us orders. I saw that the women competed to do things for him, maybe sewing a button for him or asking to polish his shoes with a bit of cloth. This was very strange to me: why they should want to go out of their way for him. The police were to be feared, not courted, even the handsome ones. The best hope was simply to stay out of their way.

Then one day—what possessed me then? It was against my nature, surely. One day, as Heniek was walking by, I suddenly blurted something out to him.

"Why are they doing this? Why are the women doing these things for you? I would never do you such favors!"

"*Smarkata*," he shot back. "Snot-nosed brat." That's the best translation I can think of. Smarkata. You say it to an unruly child, to someone who is no threat, but just a nuisance, someone whom you brush off without a second thought.

"Smarkata," he said, "you'll see, one day you'll want to do something for me, too."

And I said, "No, never."

He kept walking.

Never mind. He came, he went. We worked.

I wasn't much thinking about boys then, anyway—about men. What I was thinking about, what was ever on my mind, was food, and hunger, and danger, and death.

At first, I didn't eat. I had never been much of an eater, any-way. Perhaps this is why sandwiches made from buttered corn-bread and sliced pineapple were such a treat for me. But Hitler taught me to eat; that's what I say now. In the ghetto, meat didn't exist. We lived on bread—we were allotted one hun-dred grams per person per day—and occasionally a potato if someone was able to get one. At the factory, we were fed twice a day, once before our first six-hour shift, and once after our second. In the mornings, we got what they called coffee—though no one thought what we drank actually had any coffee in it—along with a slice of brown bread. After our twelve hours of work, there was a watery soup of some kind that sometimes had little bits of meat floating in it.

I was hungry at the factory, hungry in a way I hadn't known in the ghetto. But even though the hollow pull of hunger never left me, I knew I couldn't eat this soup. The soup was unkosher; it was *traif*. My family hadn't been especially religious—my fa-ther didn't wear a beard, and neither he nor my brother went to synagogue on Shabbos—but we followed all the observances of Jewish ritual, just as everyone around us did: We didn't work on Shabbos, the women kept their arms and legs covered, and, of course, we kept kosher. There was never a question about these things; it was how we lived and how our families had lived for as long as we knew. This soup at the factory was traif, and I knew for a certainty that if I put it to my lips, I would choke.

People around me tried to get me to relent. "You have to eat," Sally Apel said. "You need to eat whatever they will give us." But I couldn't; I couldn't put that meat in my mouth.

Until I did.

I remember taking that first spoonful. I fully expected to gag. It wasn't a lightning bolt I anticipated; I didn't think God would strike me down from above. Instead, I really thought my body would not accept the traif; I thought my throat would close up. I thought I would die.

I held my nose as I put the spoon to my tongue. I let the warm liquid linger in my mouth for a moment, and then I swallowed.

I didn't die. The broth tasted good to me, slightly salty, faintly smoky.

Maybe something broke in me then, something very small, probably unnoticeable. A Jew could not eat traif, and yet I did. Traif was supposed to be poison for a Jew, and yet this traif had not poisoned me. Was this the beginning of the end of my faith? I can't know such things. I know only that I came to crave the flavor of that traif, that barest hint of meat, that slight remembrance of real food in our daily portion of watery broth.

Some months later, I found out what it was we were eating in the soup. Every so often, some men would bring into the factory kitchen the carcass of a horse to be butchered. The main parts of the meat would go to the Germans, of course; the workers got the bits scraped off from the bones. The first time I saw a carcass brought into the kitchen—the whole animal, heavy and draped across the shoulders of two men laboring under its weight, its head slightly bobbing with each step the men took, eyes wide open and bulging, staring intently at absolutely nothing—it looked ghoulishly alive. I knew then that this was where the scraps of meat in our soup came from, and I shuddered to think that this was what I was eating, what I in fact was craving. Even now, when I see a horse trotting through a field, I see the same swollen, vacant eyes, at once focused and drained of life. I ate the soup; I learned to love it. It was food; it was life.

The days in the factory quickly became routine. I worked twelve hours at the machines, I was fed twice a day, I had a shower maybe once a month. We didn't think much about what we were doing; certainly we didn't talk about it. We were, after all, working in an armaments factory, helping our enemies, helping to make the very munitions that were being used against us. We just did our work. We did what we were told to do. We were trying to survive.

Even now, I don't know exactly what type of armament I was involved in making; the division of the factory I worked in was called the *celownik*, which means "aiming device." At first the work went very slowly; I knew my measurements had to be exact. I was always scared that the holes I drilled would be too deep or too shallow or too wide. I stopped after every other piece to measure and check, and this, of course, slowed down my pace. I didn't know how to do this kind of work. I was fifteen, small-boned, and just over five feet tall; the machine I worked at was enormous. I had to stand on a box so that I could maneuver the drill bit.

I have no idea what went through my head during all those hours. The clank and constant roar of the machines made talking impossible, and it was forbidden to speak with anyone during work, in any event. All those hours—drilling, measuring, drilling, measuring. The metal shavings that came off the slugs accumulated on my hands, became embedded in my palms, around my fingernails. My hands turned black; it took nearly a year for the flesh of my hands to return to their normal color. I was afraid of the monster of a machine I worked at—afraid of its size, its noise; I was afraid of working too slowly; I was afraid of working too fast. I was afraid of making a mistake.

I ached for Mama. Hour after hour. Day after day.

After I had spent two months at the factory, the Germans decided to make a point. I don't know why. Were we not working enough? Had someone tried to escape? Or had the Germans simply awoken that morning in the mood for murder?

It was Yom Kippur, September 1942.

A German officer came onto the factory floor. That was unusual in itself. The floor supervisor was a Pole named Zwirek. He was formal with us, but he never treated us cruelly, and he offered us some kind of buffer from the German soldiers and officers who were in control. This German's presence on the factory floor was therefore clear cause for alarm. He told us we must stop working and gather outside in the yard.

The machines were turned off, their gears and motors whirring down. Nobody spoke, though I could tell everyone was filled with questions. The place was suddenly heavy with silence: You could touch the quiet in the thickness of the air. We all left our stations and hurried together down the stairs and into the courtyard in front of the factory building. Someone—a policeman, perhaps—lined us up in rows in the yard, several hundred of us. The smaller ones, myself included, were put in the front, taller ones behind. Everyone was to watch; everyone was to see what was about to happen.

There was a man, maybe forty years old, standing about thirty feet away from us. He was tied with a thick cord to a tall wooden pole that seemed to have been set into the ground for the occasion. I didn't know him, though others around me told me he was also from Radom and that he came from a good family.

In a line in front of and facing this man were fifteen or twenty German soldiers, each holding a rifle.

The officer then addressed us.

"I know," he said, "this day you call Yom Kippur is very important for you, a day of sacrifice."

He held himself very straight, very rigid. He barely moved as he spoke.

"Today is your day of holy sacrifice," he said. "So today I have chosen a sacrifice for you. I have chosen a man, and he will be your offering."

He spoke to us flatly, without emphasis, without the slightest whiff of drama. He spoke as if he were doing us a favor, taking on himself the obligation to offer a sacrifice on a Jewish holy day.

Then he turned to the soldiers and gave a command. At his order, the soldiers lifted their rifles and took aim.

The man was bound tightly to the wooden pole, a stake in the ground like those used during the Inquisition, when people were tied to the stake and set on fire. Martyrs go to their deaths this way, bound to a stake. What could this man have been thinking then, knowing that he was about to die? I hoped absurdly that he would run, as Weinberg had. Weinberg at least was running, desperate, crazy, perhaps, to think that he might have a chance, that running could possibly mean escape. But at least Weinberg was running when he was shot; at least he got to try to avoid the bullets. But not this man. He was forced to stand and watch as his killers raised their guns to him; he had to stand and wait, even if only for seconds, for the guns to go off.

Standing in the front row, I felt the shots. I thought the bullets were hitting me; I thought I could feel each bullet slam against my body as they slammed into his. The shots were so loud, so piercing and hard, a reverberating smack of a sound in a factory courtyard.

The man buckled at the knees and crumpled down the pole.

I watched, silent, stunned. I had never before seen anyone killed at such close range. If the German officer had wanted to scare us, to let us know that he could do anything he pleased and that we must do whatever he said, he certainly accomplished his goal.

When it was over, then what? When it was over, then nothing. It was over. We were sent back to work.

I had been at the factory for maybe two months, and in that time, I had seen two men murdered—one supposedly for sabotage, the other, I supposed, to scare us into compliance. Though I had been sent to the factory to live, the murder of these two men made me realize that I, too, would die, that the work I was given to perform might delay, but would not prevent, my death. I didn't precisely give up on life; it's important to understand this. I didn't invite death, as some people did, especially later in Auschwitz. But at some point, I simply understood with a certainty that astonished me that my death was inevitable. And what consumed me, what made me afraid, was not the fact of my dying, but its manner. Would it hurt? Would it be quick? Would I have to stand and watch as soldiers raised their rifles to me? Once these questions entered my mind, I couldn't let them go, or to be more accurate, they wouldn't let go of me. I thought of these questions always. Will it hurt? Will I be in pain when I die?

I was a girl of fifteen. I was not courageous. What should I have been thinking of?

Soon after the Yom Kippur "sacrifice," I had my own encounter with death. It came when I made a mistake I was not allowed to make.

Zwirek, the Pole who supervised the celownik, came up to me one evening as I started to work at my machine. He had never spoken to me or addressed me in any way before. Sometimes when he passed by in front of my row of machines, I could see that he was smiling slightly, as if he were indicating his approval of my work. But I didn't want his attention; I wanted to stay hidden.

He was trim and fit, I remember, and very tall; I reached just below his shoulders.

"I have to speak to you," he said, quietly and without anger, but firmly, too, with some urgency.

What could he mean? What could he possibly want to speak to me about?

He continued, "Do you know what you did?"

What did I do? What could I have done? I always did as I was told: I stood on my little box in front of the enormous machine and drilled holes, for twelve hours a day, six days a week.

"You know," he said, "all the fifteen hundred pieces that you made last night—they are no good. Every one you put in the box is wrong."

Out of the fifteen hundred pieces I was required to drill each shift, I was allowed maybe two or three that weren't right. The rest had to be precise, perfect.

"What happened?" he asked. "You know what's going to be done. You know what this means."

What could I say? I didn't know what happened. I was tired, maybe; I fell asleep at the machine; I was sick. Who knows? I worked vacantly—maybe my hands drilled holes without my head knowing what I was doing.

I said, "I cannot give you an answer; I don't know what happened. I can't even make up an excuse."

It was a death sentence. I had seen Weinberg shot for committing sabotage. Zwirek had said to me, "You know what this means," and I knew precisely what it meant: It meant my execution. Zwirek said these words to me, and I saw in my mind young Weinberg falling to the ground with bullets in his back.

I don't think I was afraid. I was numb.

Zwirek was shaking a little, I remember, staring down at me. I remember wondering for a moment if he was trembling from anger or something else. And then suddenly I could see in his eyes that he actually pitied me, that he hated this situation that we were in, that he wanted to figure out something to do.

He said quietly, "I cannot let you die. I cannot let you die. But I don't know what there is to do." And then he left. He simply turned away from me and went back to his office, and I turned back to the machine and to my work, trying to drill each hole precisely right.

Later that night, Zwirek came back and took me aside. I remember I had to bend my neck all the way back to look up at him standing over me.

"I will take these boxes," he said, softly, almost tenderly, "and I will bring them back to my office. And for every box that you finish, I will take out some good ones and put back in some of these bad ones. And I will substitute these for those until all the mistakes are gone. But you mustn't make any more mistakes. The rest have to be perfect."

Then, without waiting for a reply, he left, and he never spoke to me again.

For nothing, a man was killed; for nothing, my life was saved.

Zwirek was a Pole; I was a Jew. That is important.

༄

How is it possible to discover love in a place like this? I am speaking here not of sex, though surely there was that, too, in the barracks—people fumbling under clothes, softly moaning on the bunks, intertwining, needing not to care that others were around. No, not this, though I think perhaps I understood even then how strong sexual desire can be. But this is not the love I mean. Or, to be true, not only this. It is more mysterious to me, my love for Heniek. It felt older than anything, an ancient connection awakened in a terrible time, maybe because of the terror of the time.

Let me think, let me think: Can I pinpoint the beginning of my love? It wasn't when I first saw him, that I know. Heniek was a ladies' man, as I have said, dashing and confident when he swept into the barracks to check in on the women. We were called the armaments workers, but really, we were slaves, half starving, beyond exhausted; no one had more than a single change of clothes. When had anyone last brushed her teeth? Set her hair? And yet when Heniek came in, smartly put together with his policeman's cap and his polished boots, he spoke to us as if we were women—real, true women and not the bedraggled creatures we surely were. His gentle flatteries—they were innocuous, offhand, but for that, all the more charming—they endeared him to us. Over time, I started to realize why the women might have wanted to do him small favors, to be noticed by a man like this, to be desired even by a good man—no one ever spoke ill of Heniek, not during the war and not after—and to be noticed in a place like this.

But not for me. Heniek's attentions were not for me; I was the smarkata. A kid, a fifteen-year-old brat. I wasn't worth his notice.

But later . . . when? Some months, maybe; surely after Zwirek had saved my life. I find my mind is filled with him. Heniek comes into the barracks to escort a group to the factory compound a couple of kilometers away, and the air about me feels charged, electric. A young girl's infatuation with an older and striking man—I suppose I have to admit that. I suppose that must be some part of it. But that is not all of it; it isn't only that.

I am lying in my bunk; it's Sunday, maybe, a day without work at the factory. There is nothing to do, nothing to expect. The women in the barracks are shuffling about; some go to the latrine to rinse out their clothes, some are softly chatting. Everyone is hungry; everyone is withered from exhaustion. It is a day of emptiness like every other. Then, in my bunk, thinking of nothing, staring at nothing, I feel something inside me stir. Deep beyond anything I can touch, deep down in the pit of my stomach, something comes alive. I am up, out of my bunk, and at the window. I look past the grime on the glass and out into the desolate yard. There's no one there, just the dust of the ground, and the other barracks beyond. Then suddenly Heniek comes into view. My heart races at the sight of him.

But how did I know? How did I know that Heniek was near?

I keep my heart in hiding. Heniek must not know this young girl is drawn to him. I don't understand this feeling that has overtaken me, consumed me. That I want him near. That I can feel it when he's near. I don't know where it came from.

When I was younger, twelve, maybe, or thirteen, I sometimes would sneak into the corner of the courtyard outside our apartment building on Wolnosc Street and sit with my friends, girls and boys both, and we would exchange playing cards on which were printed little love notes. "I like the way you look." "I would like to walk with you to school." "I think your dress is pretty." We passed them around amid giggles and bashful eyes. It was innocent, daringly risqué, and hugely fun. This is what I knew of boys and girls—playing cards in a courtyard. It was exciting enough.

Now, in the factory, it's different. I'm just fifteen—barely out of pigtails and entirely innocent of the ways of men and women. Yet I dream of Heniek kissing me, holding me, running his fingers through my baby-fine hair.

One day, Heniek catches my eye as we stand outside the barracks. I look away, unsure of what I'm supposed to do. But I see him smile.

One day, when Heniek comes to escort the women to the factory, he positions himself near me so that we walk side by side down the road. My skin tingles; something dances deep inside.

One day, Heniek finds me alone outside the barracks, and he takes my hand.

In such a place, Heniek takes my hand. I have never before been touched by a man; I had thought that if I touched a boy, I would get pregnant. But standing outside the rough-hewn barracks of a slave-labor factory, with no one around, so no one can see, Heniek takes my hand, softly, firmly, and it feels as though I have been shot through by lightning. I feel Heniek's touch along every inch of me. I feel luminous, alive, radiant with desire.

কও

Our courtship lasted several months. Heniek would wait for me to finish my shift at the factory, and I would catch sight of him standing there at the bottom of the factory stairwell looking up for me, searching me out among all the women finally released from their labor. After twelve numbing hours drilling metal, I'd see Heniek's face, at once eager and assured, and suddenly there would be this little throbbing inside me, a delicate, pulsing warmth running in my veins. That feeling! The thrill of it! Twelve hours at the machine, and then Heniek as my reward.

He would tell me how beautiful I was, how sweet my eyes, my skin, he said, like the petals of a rose—and I would run back to the barracks at night to find my reflection in the dirty glass of the window, hoping to see what he saw, hoping to discover that beauty, that sweetness for myself. I thought if I could glimpse the beauty he so admired, I might be assured of his love; I might know that there was something lasting there, something that couldn't be taken away.

Heniek told me one day he intended to take me dancing. I shouldn't worry, he said; he would see to everything.

A refined and elegant gentleman asks his young girlfriend on a date—a rendezvous in town at a small local restaurant, where there is polished cutlery on the table and perhaps a candle to set the mood. Waiters in suits come by to set down plates with thick hunks of meat robed in a glistening sauce; the potatoes taste of butter. At the far end of the room, a man in a bow tie plays at an old upright piano, and the couple pauses from their meal and walks hand in hand to the center of the floor. The man places his hand on the small of his lady's back—she is such a delicate thing, he can feel each of her ribs under her loose-fitting dress—and he presses her gently toward him as the pianist plays his tune. And the young lady rests her head on his broad shoulder and feels his strength under the softness of her cheek.

Heniek took me dancing. It feels like a dream. My head forgets—how did we manage to leave the compound without being noticed? How did we manage to walk through the streets of Radom and eat at a Polish restaurant and not look like the Jews we were? I don't know these things. But the body remembers when the mind forgets. I remember in my body, in my bones, the feeling of my night out with Heniek, dancing with Heniek—his hand on my back, my cheek pressed against his chest, the quiver in my legs.

I had removed my armband. Heniek had taken off his policeman's cap. He told me not to be frightened. We danced as if getting caught wouldn't mean our death.

I was petrified.

I was in love.

Everything Heniek and I shared was secret, all our time together stolen. Yet nothing could have felt more sanctioned or ordained.

I was in love with Heniek Greenspan, and for a short time, I was not alone.

4

HENIEK ASKED ME TO GO WITH HIM TO ARGENTINA.

By this time, I had been working in the kitchen for six months or more. It was one of Heniek's many gifts to me to get me added to the kitchen staff; I don't know how he managed it. But Heniek had some prestige, and not only among the women. He was liked; he had friends. Maybe he called in a favor; maybe he paid someone off; maybe—maybe—someone thought to do him a good turn.

The kitchen was heaven compared with the factory floor. It is important here to get the emphasis right: heaven not in itself, no, not in the least. I sat on a stool between two beer barrels, and it was my job to peel potatoes—two hundred kilos of them—every day. How many potatoes is that? I wonder. A thousand, maybe? One thousand potatoes a day. Not counting the rotten ones, that's maybe a potato to peel every minute, twelve hours every day, six days a week, for over a year. My fingers grew cramped gripping the gnarled and knotty shapes in one hand and the slim handle of a small paring knife in the other. The cramps would come after maybe a half hour of work in the morning. Between every few potatoes, I'd take a moment, a second merely, to stretch my fingers to try to relieve the pain jabbing in my joints, but it never went away, not really. The knife I used was more precious to me than anything; I guarded it more keenly than I guarded myself. If I lost that knife, if someone stole it, I would have had to peel those potatoes with my nails. I wore the blade down almost to a sliver. I slept with it every night, tucked under Mama's feather blanket.

So not a heaven in itself, but heaven in comparison to the factory floor. In the kitchen, I worked only during the days. I got to work beside four other women filling their own quota of peeled potatoes, and I got to sit with them around a potbellied stove that staved off the worst of the winter cold. When we were alone in the kitchen, we could chat quietly among ourselves, though about what I do not know. One of the girls—it pains me that I do not remember her name—had a lovely, delicate voice, and sometimes she would sweetly sing, Jewish songs mostly, and we would sing along in a hush, as best we could. Every now and then, if we were certain no one was near, we might even shave off a thin slice of potato and slap it against the outside of the stove so it would stick. We'd let it cook for a moment or two, then carefully peel it off and eat it, an illicit indulgence, a secret treat. A chip.

These comforts, these minor pleasures—the barest hints of normality—I owed to Heniek, who had done I-don't-know-what to get me there.

Heniek came into the kitchen every now and then, as I have said. It was at the end of my work shift one day that he told me he had something to discuss and we should go outside.

It was getting dark, and he spoke to me in the shadows of the fading light outside the kitchen building. It was hard to understand what he was saying, what he was proposing. It was so wild a thought, so drastic, so miraculous, so frightening.

Heniek told me that the Germans were organizing an exchange. Anyone with Argentinean citizenship living in Poland would be allowed to leave with his or her family and return to South America; Argentina, in turn, would presumably release any German nationals living there. Heniek himself was Polish, of course, but his sister had married a man with Argentinean citizenship, and this man, Heniek's brother-in-law, had offered to register Heniek as his brother. Heniek would then be able to take his own family with him and escape to South America. Heniek was proposing to take me. He was proposing that we get married.

Outside a barracks kitchen in the diminishing light, hidden in the shadows so that no one will see, I feel faint at Heniek's side, suddenly overtaken by an idea I don't fully understand, by questions I don't know fully how to frame. To escape this! And with Heniek! To be with him, to go someplace safe, someplace not here. To live a life, to go where we please. Might there really be a future, Heniek, for me? Might there be a future, Heniek, for us?

But Argentina. Where is this place? Far, far away—this I know. Across a wide expanse of sea, another world entirely. I have heard stories, Heniek, from my childhood. Bedtime horror stories about this place. Men come to Europe from

Argentina, and they entice girls off the streets and lure them back to South America and turn them into whores. How can I go to a place like that? And can I leave my family behind? Mima and Feter, and my father, too—there are so few left to me. Am I to desert them?

I need to think; I need to find a resting place from the dizzying swirl of questions in my head. I should be back in the courtyard exchanging playing cards with my friends. I should be back on Wolnosc Street helping Mama make Friday night dinners. I should be spending my nights warm beside her, pestering her to make me a new dress. How am I to make a decision like this? I'm only sixteen; I don't know how I am supposed to figure this out.

I must get to the ghetto, to see my aunt and uncle and my father. I need to ask them what I should do.

ויזצ

I sit here now from this long distance across the decades, trying to understand how the mind of a young girl goes. I am trying to find her, to ask her how this plan, this proposed exchange, could have made sense. But it wasn't just me, of course; it was all of us—what we were willing to believe, what we willed ourselves not to know.

To be fair, there had been a precedent, two even. I think it's fair to say that there were two.

A Radomer woman who had immigrated to Mandate Palestine before the war had returned to Poland at some point on a British visa. Golda Graucher was her name. She had two sons with her, but one of them—Natan Chaim, just ten years old—

had died while they were in Poland. Sometime before Heniek spoke to me about the exchange with Argentina—it might even have been a year before—Mrs. Graucher had been allowed by the Germans to return to Palestine, and she had managed to take with her a ten-year-old Radomer boy, Eli Gottlieb, on her dead son's visa. So here was an example of the Germans letting someone, even a Jew, with a foreign visa leave the country.

Did I think of this story then? This boy was Eli Gottlieb, not Natan Chaim Graucher, and yet he had made it out of Poland. Did I reason it out, that if they let Eli Gottlieb leave, they might also let me leave? Eli Gottlieb made it to Palestine, changed his name to Eliyahu Ben-Elissar, earned advanced degrees at the University of Paris and the University of Geneva after the war, and eventually became the first Israeli ambassador to Egypt. All this because he had managed to escape Radom by pretending he had both a nationality status and a name that weren't in fact his own.

Then, too, there were those from Argentina itself. There was a young girl I knew from the ghetto; her name, I remember, was Henia Friedman. I later found out that she was part of Heniek's brother-in-law's extended family, but I didn't know that, of course, in the ghetto. I knew she had been born on a boat in Argentinean waters and that she therefore had Argentinean citizenship. I don't imagine I understood what that meant in any official way, but I knew that citizenship gave her certain privileges in the ghetto. She was not required to wear the armband bearing the Magen David that identified us as Jews. She was able to keep—and even to wear—her leather coat. And she was allowed to leave the ghetto without getting specific permission. It was astonishing to us that she could come and go through those ghetto gates, that she could pass by the police standing guard there, without any problem at all. It was as if she weren't even a Jew, as if she were free.

So there was some logic here. I have to believe that logic played some part in our readiness to accept that this exchange could take place and that some number of Jews would be allowed to leave.

༺༄༻

Heniek arranged for me to return to the ghetto one afternoon. Another policeman escorted me there—I wouldn't, of course, be allowed to go alone, and I preferred not to go this time with Heniek. The policeman left me at the ghetto gates and told me to meet him there a couple of hours later. That's what I would have—two hours to figure out my future, two hours to decide if I should leave what family I had remaining to me, leave the only place I had ever known, and travel across what seemed a limitless ocean to a place I had barely heard of.

My family seemed to think there was less to discuss than I did. No one asked me if I loved Heniek, if I would be happy trying to build a life with this man who had asked to marry me. That didn't matter. Only one thing mattered—that the exchange was a way out of Radom, out of Poland, out of the war.

"Go," Feter said. "If you have a chance to go, then you must go."

Feter had thrown me out of the apartment in the ghetto the year before, to force me to return to the factory; now he was pushing me out of the country.

They were desperate, I see that now. Since almost the entire population of the ghetto had been deported, rumors had begun to spread about what deportation meant. A Pole had been paid to follow a train on his bicycle to see where the trains went. Jews were taken from Radom on trucks; from trucks they were loaded onto trains. But where did the trains go? The Pole returned with news of a camp of some kind near Treblinka village. He had heard it was a place where Jews were killed—gassed or shot, hundreds at a time. He had heard that thousands of Jews entered the camp, but none ever left.

Feter must have been thinking of this Pole. My uncle was adamant. I must go. He must have been desperate to keep me from Treblinka. Perhaps, too, he was thinking of his own daughter; perhaps he was thinking of Chava.

Chava had been killed the year before.

Chava had been petrified living in the ghetto. She was six years old and wracked by nightmares in that cramped room on Szwarlikowska Street. She would wake in the night, clutching at her mother and screaming—shrieking, really—"The Germans are coming! The Germans are going to kill me!" Mima would gather her up in her arms, stroke her hair, and try to lull her gently to sleep.

"Hush, my child, hush. Everything will be all right."

Mama and I, in the next bed, would return to sleep to the sound of Chava's whimpers.

Feter, I think, was more aware than the rest of us of how truly dangerous the ghetto was. More than the rest of us, he was always working to see if he could find a way out for the family. He had made that trip to Russia early in the war to try to arrange passage for Mima and their children. When he returned to Radom after that didn't work, he eventually found and paid a Polish family to hide his children—Chava and Moishele—for the duration of the war. Both were too young to be accepted for work, and so both were in special danger. He knew how frightened Chava was living in the ghetto. Chava and Moishele lived with the Polish family for some months—perhaps even half a year—but several days before the large deportations in the summer of 1942, the woman of this family came to the ghetto to give the children back. She must have heard that the deportations were coming and decided it was too dangerous to shelter Jewish children.

Desperate and with no other options available, Feter decided to hide his children at the local tannery where he worked. By this time, Feter had already forced me out of the apartment to work in the factory; he told me what had happened only later, after it was all over.

When the deportations came, Feter had the children with him in the tannery. They were hiding somewhere near him, though I don't think he told me precisely where. Perhaps they were secreted in a closet; perhaps they cowered behind a heap of leather. When the Germans entered the building to search for anyone not supposed to be there—like children—Chava suddenly found her nightmares coming true. The Germans had come, and they were going to kill her. All of six years old and terrified for her life, she bolted from her hiding place and ran.

She was caught, of course, before she could even get out of the building. Feter watched as his daughter was grabbed up by a soldier and carried out, kicking her legs and crying out to her father for help.

Later that day, Feter was told by a friend what happened next. The tannery abutted a small park called the Peltze Guten, and there the Germans had dug—or, more likely, had

had their workers dig—a large ditch. The soldier threw Chava into this ditch, and then he threw in a grenade.

Was Feter thinking of Treblinka when he told me one year later to go to Argentina with Heniek, a man he barely knew? When he told me that I must get as far away from Poland as I could, was he thinking of Chava?

My two hours were up. There was no debate. Feter announced it, and Mima and my father agreed: I had to go.

I returned to the barracks and found Heniek. I was frightened, of course, frightened of everything—of the venture, of leaving my family, of being a wife at sixteen. But I was excited, too; I must acknowledge this—I was excited for the vibrant possibility of it all, for the joy of saying yes.

Yes, Heniek, yes. Yes, I will marry you. Yes, I will go with you to Argentina.

Heniek took me in his arms and looked at me with such a searching gladness in his eyes that I really did believe that we could escape that place and live together somewhere in deep and unburdened love. And then he kissed me on my lips—a wondrous, lingering kiss. I pledged myself to him and he to me—that we would love each other always, wherever we would be. And I was happy—it is so hard to say this, even now, even after everything—I was happy in my Heniek's arms.

We agreed on a date, just a few days later. We would be married.

I returned to the ghetto one more time to get a ring. My family thought it important that I be able to give Heniek something.

Not a dowry exactly, but some material token of my family's thanks for the escape Heniek was offering me. Feter gave me a little money, and I went to a friend of the family's, a goldsmith named Menashe Friedman, who had managed to keep a small, secret business going in his ghetto apartment. I asked him to make a ring for me—a band with Heniek's initials, HG, engraved in low relief on the outside.

Menashe didn't want to take my money; it seemed he wanted me. He said he would make the ring for free, only, he said, I mustn't go to Argentina.

"Don't marry this man. Don't leave Radom. You want to give him a ring; give him. But don't leave Radom with him."

Was he thinking of my safety? Was he suspicious of the proposed exchange? Later, after the war, I was in touch with his sister, and she told me that her mother was always talking about me, saying that I would be a good match for her son the goldsmith. But I had no knowledge of this then, and it wouldn't have made any difference to me, anyway. I was interested only in Heniek, and I was marrying him despite the idea of escaping to Argentina, not because of it.

People in the barracks seemed to want me not to go as well. They wanted to take my place; one woman offered me a fortune if I would give up my place in the exchange to her (I told her to ask Heniek; it wasn't up to me whom he would take). And they wondered why Heniek had picked *me*. What was so special about me that among all the women working at the factory—there were nearly five hundred of us—Heniek had asked me to go with him?

What could I say? I didn't know myself what he saw in me. There were women in the barracks who were more educated than I, who came from wealthier homes. I had been the smarkata, and yet Heniek had chosen me, me among all the others. Perhaps because I was young? He was twenty-eight at the time. He told me once that a friend joked with him that he was robbing the cradle in marrying me, that I was too young to know anything, and he joked back that his friend shouldn't worry—he would raise me right. So maybe my youth was appealing to him, just as his worldly maturity appealed to me. Whatever it was, I was gladdened by his choice, proud even, if I can say it, that among all the women wanting him, Heniek wanted me.

Heniek and I were married several days later in Mima and Feter's single room on Szwarlikowska Street. My father was there, but it was Feter who said the blessings. We shared a sip of something, though I don't know what, and Heniek broke a glass. We had no documents to sign. We had no *ketubah*, and we had, of course, no marriage license from the state.

This is what even now I struggle to make sense of: How did we think this was going to work? Heniek did not have the same last name as his brother-in-law; I never had any document to share a name with Heniek. I was Mania Drezner before I got married and I was Mania Drezner after. So how did we think we could be convincingly claimed as part of Heniek's brother-in-law's family? I don't understand this. Something doesn't make sense here in the story of my own life; there's a blank space in my history, and I have no way to fill it in and no one to ask.

Nonetheless, we were married. Heniek gave me a simple gold band, and I gave him the ring I had gotten made for him with his initials engraved on top.

I have the rings still. Both rings, tied together with a thin length of thread.

Sometime later, we had a picture taken. Try as I might—and it bothers me that there are things that stay hidden in me somewhere, inaccessible to my searching, whereas others I remember with a readiness that amazes me—I cannot recall where or when or how we got this picture taken. But I have it even now, along with the rings. It's black and white, of course, and we look—I need to say this—we look happy, almost eager. Our temples are touching, my face slightly lower than his, and we're both looking straight at the camera. I am smiling slightly, even a little impishly. I remember I didn't like how my hair looked in the picture—it's done up in a way, as if supported by curlers, and I still think I don't look good in it. It's printed on flimsy paper; all the edges are frayed, and there are jagged creases down the middle because of the way it was kept when I was at Auschwitz. But it's a lovely picture, nonetheless.

All through my life, during the many decades that followed, I have kept this picture with me. Years after the war, Jack mounted it on a little rectangle of cardboard to give it some substance. How sweet this was of Jack, how selfless, to pre-

serve a picture of me with another man. But I put the picture away: It stays in an old envelope on a shelf in the back of my closet hidden behind my clothes. Wherever I have lived—in Germany after the war, in various apartments and houses in New York after we came to America—I have kept this picture, secretly close to my heart, but tucked away.

Our evening was over. We had to return to the factory—Heniek to his duties in the police, I to my work in the kitchen. We would be leaving shortly for Argentina.

Soon thereafter, we got word: The "exchange" had taken place. Seventeen people, all related in a single family—Heniek's sister and brother-in-law, the girl Henia Friedman, all those who were designated for the exchange with Germans living in Argentina—were gathered together in the ghetto and taken to the central square, presumably for transport. But then, instead of being loaded onto trucks, they were lined up and shot. We heard that one member of the family escaped: Heniek's nephew, Amek Bleiweis, somehow knowing not to trust the reality of the exchange, lowered himself into the dugout of a communal latrine and hid in human excrement until the massacre was over. He said the stench stayed on him for weeks. Heniek and I eluded the slaughter, but for no reason other than that we were not living in or visiting the ghetto when it happened.

This was the maniacal logic of the war. I couldn't understand it then, and it's certainly no clearer to me now, why the Germans thought it necessary to concoct this ruse. The Germans were killing us routinely and without cause. My brother was shot because he had a limp. Chava had been murdered because she was running in fear. Rafalowitz and Weinberg and the man the German officer killed at the factory on Yom Kippur: The Germans didn't need a reason; they killed because they killed. So why did they need a story about people going to Argentina in order to kill them? Was the story to worsen the pain? To deliver people to death only after giving them the hope of life?

And why had we been spared? This is a different sort of question, I know. But it was a question that haunted me. I had visited the ghetto just a day or two before the killing. I could have been there. I could have been killed. For no reason at all, Heniek and I were simply elsewhere when the killing occurred. So we were alive.

At least then. At least at that point.

இ

Heniek and I were married in idea, really, more than in actuality. We couldn't live together, of course, and we barely had time alone. Heniek had a room in one of the barracks—a wooden bed, a thin mattress, a standing lamp without a shade. I don't know whether the room was his or if he somehow got permission to use someone else's for an hour or two at a time. We didn't go there much; it was against the rules, and I had to walk back to my barracks in the dark on my own. And there was always fear, always the threat of getting caught.

Heniek was twelve years older than I; he knew how to handle himself in the world, he had experience of women, and he had a good deal of power over the Jews in his charge. I was young and vulnerable and innocent of absolutely everything. I gave myself to Heniek, and he could have done with me whatever he pleased. But what pleased Heniek was to be a gentleman. Heniek loved me with patience and with tenderness, and he guided me gently with his kisses to find my deepest pleasure.

In the end, we were married for only a short time. Perhaps just a few months, though truly, I don't know. I don't myself know when exactly we got married, and there is no legal record of the date. Perhaps we were married in the summer of 1943; perhaps it was the fall. I cannot say how

long Heniek Greenspan was my husband; I know only that
it was not long enough.

꾸꾸

In the winter of 1943–1944, the area of the barracks on
Skolzna Street became a *Konzentrationslager*, a concentration
camp. A few months earlier, in November 1943, the Radom
ghetto was finally emptied and my aunt and uncle came to the
factory with their son, Moishele. He was still too young to
work, but they tried as best they could to make him look older,
and he managed to survive almost another year, until we were
sent to Auschwitz.

Once the barracks became a *KL*, any sense we had that
working in the factory would protect us vanished. A double
row of barbed-wire fencing was erected around the perimeter
of the barracks; the wires were electrified so anyone who
touched them would die. We were given uniforms, the striped
dresses that you see in pictures—dirty gray and blue stripes
and cloth so coarse it scratched whenever it touched your
skin. We were allowed to keep whatever clothes we had from
the ghetto, but we had to wear the uniforms every day. And
there were new rules. We were told: "Do not try to escape. If
anyone escapes, twenty will be killed in their place."

The Germans were true to their word. Some people did
escape. People were killed on account of them. And Heniek
and I got caught up in the whole horror of it. Another Jewish
policeman, Duvid Norembursky, was one of those who escaped; he was responsible for my Heniek's death.

5

EVERYTHING NOW BEGINS TO HAPPEN VERY FAST. THE EVENTS of the winter of 1943–1944 all happened in such quick succession, they exist in my memory as multiple strands of a single story. But it is not at all clear to me how precisely the strands are intertwined—how precisely they relate to each other, in time and in cause. I know them only as I feel them: filaments of grief and fear woven deeply into my life.

తుంది

In the weeks immediately before and after the creation of the Konzentrationslager at the barracks on Skolzna Street, it was clear that life in the ghetto was getting ever more precarious. It wasn't only I who thought the factory barracks were safer than the ghetto streets. Even despite its own brand of horrors, the barracks provided some measure of protection. The roundups were fewer; the food—though only hard bread and thin broth flecked with meat—was at least distributed every day. We were comforted with what we forced ourselves to believe: that the Germans needed us to work, that they wouldn't kill us if we worked.

In the ghetto, people longed for work at the factory. The liquidations had emptied the ghetto of most of its inhabitants; those who remained were desperate to devise ways to leave and work for the war. Duvid Norembursky, a member of the ghetto police, was one of those who found a way.

I have much to say about Duvid Norembursky; he is the villain of my story. But I need to admit that I cannot be objective about the man: I do not know what was in his heart; I do not know what in fact linked the series of events that I will describe. What I can say with certainty is that this is how we in the factory understood these events; this is how we—and not I alone—put them together to tell a story that made sense, however horrendous it was.

෨෨

There was a foundry, a *kuznia*, connected to the ammunitions factory, a place of fire and smoke and molten-hot metals. Working there was one of the most feared assignments in the compound. People had to inhale sooty air for twelve hours every day, blackening their lungs, dying from within. What precisely they did there—make gun parts, repair machines— truly, I do not know. But nobody ever wanted to work there, especially the girls.

The kuznia was run by a German officer named Commandant Miller. Hundreds of men and women worked in the kuznia, of course, but Miller also chose young girls to work specifically for him. There were fifty, I think, from Radom whom he selected. He looked for a certain kind of girl—healthy, young, robust. The girls were petrified to be chosen. I knew a girl who cut off two of her fingers in order to get out from under Miller's control. She claimed it was an accident, that her fingers had gotten mangled by accident while she was working at one of the kuznia's machines, but we all knew that she mutilated herself on purpose to make herself distasteful to this man.

How dreadful does a situation have to be for someone to force her fingers into the moving parts of a machine in order to escape it?

I shudder to think what went on in the kuznia, what happened with Miller when the girls weren't working at the fire. What did I know of such things?

One day, a friend of mine came into our barracks crying. I know this girl's name—I even know where she now lies buried in New York—but I won't say her name here. I don't know if she ever told her family what happened in the kuznia, and what if her children don't know this part of their mother's history? It's not for me to let it out. I respect her memory, and I will keep her name.

When she came into the barracks crying, she was barely able to speak. She took me into a corner, grasping my arms and trying to steady her breath. It was hard for her to get the words out. She started to tell me the things Miller made the girls do, what he did to them. As hard as it was for her to speak, it was as hard for me to hear. I didn't understand, really, what she was talking about. It's not just that I didn't have any experience of these things myself; it's that I didn't even know that they existed. I didn't know such perversity was in the world. This, in a way, is what the war was for us—a constant confrontation with a reality we had never imagined, never knew was even possible.

Miller made this girl take off all her clothes in front of him and stretch out over a chair. He took out a rubber baton, the truncheon he used to beat people into compliance, and he pushed it down her throat to keep her quiet. And then, as he held the baton in place, his rough hand over her mouth, the poor girl choking on the thing, coughing for air, he undid his own clothes and spread her legs and forced himself on her. Neither of us had the word for this: Do you understand? I didn't know what rape was; I didn't know there was such a thing in the world. Still, I could sense what my friend was try-ing to tell me, this horrible, unspeakable thing. My friend was telling me a story she had no words for, a lovely, innocent girl broken by a brutal man, and there was nothing I could do to help her, to make her misery go away.

I visit her grave sometimes, and I think about this story I have never told anyone, and I hope in my heart she somehow found peace.

They must have known what Miller was doing. The ghetto police. They must have been aware that Miller was sexually abusing the girls. He wasn't allowed to, not because abuse was forbidden—of course not—but because he was thereby com-mitting *Rassenschande*; literally, the word means "race shame," but it was used to describe sexual relations between a German and a Jew. Miller was mixing Aryan blood with Jewish blood, jeopardizing the purity of the master race.

Duvid Norembursky somehow knew of Miller's misdeeds.

Did the policeman spend his days scheming? Did he sit with the other members of the ghetto police, relishing the telling of his tale, a story that he must have hoped would win him favor in the eyes of Miller's superiors and would thereby benefit him and his family? Did it matter to him that his scheme would also likely send others to their doom? Surely it's clear from what he did after Heniek was taken away that Norembursky was a heartless man, that he was out only for his own safety, and to hell with the others. To hell with Heniek, to hell with the twelve additional members of the factory police who were taken away because of him, to hell even with his wife's own family. Duvid Norembursky was responsible for the death of them all.

Miller may have been all-powerful in the kuznia, but even he couldn't get away with committing Rassenschande. Cavorting with the impure Jewish race was strictly forbidden. At least this is what Norembursky must have thought. So Norembursky went to Miller's superiors in the SD, the Sicherheitsdienst—the Security Service—and reported Miller. It is important to understand that nothing Norembursky did then or afterward suggests that he was trying to protect the girls; he was trying to make himself look good to the Germans. A Jew acting on behalf of the Germans: a Jewish policeman protecting the purity of the German race. For this great act, Norembursky was in fact rewarded: He and his family, along with twelve other policemen in his group from the ghetto, along with their families, were all brought to the Konzentrationslager to stay. For reporting this crime, this group of policemen was granted the better position of working in the KL, which is precisely what it seems they wanted to achieve.

But their safety meant others' demise. The factory permitted only a certain number of policemen to work there. For the thirteen who came in from the ghetto, thirteen policemen from the factory were taken away: Heniek was one of them.

He must have known it was coming.

There was competition among the various factions of police. Heniek worked in the factory for one supervisor; the police who worked in the ghetto were responsible to someone else. Miller had his own police. Every commander reigned within his own little fiefdom, everyone trying to protect what he could. Tannenbaum, who also worked for the SD, was given a small apartment in the barracks for himself, his wife, their twins, and their maid. This is why Tannenbaum felt he was different from everyone else; he was protected, he thought, by the German commander he worked for.

But not Heniek. Heniek wasn't protected. Or not enough.

He came to me one day in the kitchen. He took me over to the corner and stood with his back to the others in the room. I was happy to see him, of course; I always was. But it made me nervous to be taken away from my work like this. I didn't know what he wanted. And what if someone saw?

He reached into his pocket and pulled something out for me to take. It was a small packet of money. He said he wanted me to have it. But why should he want me to hold his money? Why shouldn't he keep it himself? Why did he think it would be safer with me?

"No," I told him. "I don't want to hold this money; you keep it."

"It's not to hold, Maniusia; it's to keep. The money is for you. It's a gift, for whenever you will need it."

I continued to resist, but he became insistent: "You must take this, Maniusia. Maybe it will help you."

He was holding my hands, looking at me with his sweet love, imploring me to take his money, as if my taking it might give him some assurance that I would manage, that this young girl he had tried to rescue could still be saved even if he could not.

He must have had some premonition. The gift was his way of saying good-bye.

He took off his wedding ring and placed it in my palm.

We said nothing to each other about what any of this meant.

I took Heniek's money and I took his ring.

I used the money not long thereafter. The rings—Heniek's and mine both—I tied together with some thread, and later that night, I put them away in a little pocket my mother had sewn into my cloth panties. I kept them there, in my panties, until the day I arrived at Auschwitz.

Several days later, the SD came to take Heniek and the other factory policemen away. Their families, too. I was maybe twenty feet from Heniek when they grabbed him on the grounds of the KL, but I couldn't get to him. I couldn't approach him; I couldn't say good-bye. I stood twenty feet away from my husband and watched the SD lead him and the other factory police out the gates of the Konzentrationslager.

It was wintertime, and it was very cold.

Norembursky was standing there, too, watching with what looked like satisfaction as the policemen were taken away. As he passed, Heniek turned, glared at Norembursky hard in the eyes, and spoke. I heard his words distinctly; I can recite them: "Duvid," he said, "I know this is your doing. I know this is because of you." Norembursky just stood there, impassive, unmoved. He had gotten his way, no matter the cost.

What might Norembursky have felt then? What went through his mind when Heniek accused him so? They had been at school together. They had known each other for years. Did it cost Norembursky in any way to let Heniek die as he did? Did part of him, even a little bit, die, too? Part of his humanity, part of his soul? Or was it simply a victory for him to have taken someone's place? Was there only triumph now in this man's heart, that he had managed to survive?

I never saw Heniek again, and I was never able to find out what happened to him, where the Germans took him when they left the compound. Did they shoot him right there, in the streets outside the KL grounds? Did he get sent to a camp to be worked to death? To Auschwitz, perhaps, or to Treblinka? Perhaps he starved to death. Perhaps he was gassed.

Was he beaten?

Did he suffer? Did my Heniek suffer?

אמא

Heniek was my first love. For sixty years, I was married to Jack and I loved him. Jack was my everything—my strength, my purpose, my partner in life. But Heniek was my first love. There was nothing normal about our love—we courted under the eyes of our enemies; we married as a means of escape. We were husband and wife for only a few months; we never had a home, never dreamed of a family. Nothing normal, but maybe for all that, nothing ordinary. I was sixteen and in love with a charming and beautiful man, a man who had chosen me out of hundreds of women, a man who made me feel vibrant and alive in the midst of war. I was alone and frightened in a dangerous place, and Heniek entered my life to protect me and love me and teach me the fullness of pleasure. He was the center of my life. His love woke me in the morning, sustained me during the hours of empty labor, and sent me to sleep at night. He cared for me and looked out for my needs. He got me into the kitchen, where I could sit during my shifts, where I didn't have to listen all day to the screech of the drilling machines, where I could occasionally sneak a slice of potato. He spoke to me with the knowing calm of a mature man, a man I could admire without restraint. Heniek loved me with a sweet and assured warmth that I had never known before, and with all the intensity of a young girl awakening into adulthood, I loved him back. I loved him. I did.

I loved Heniek Greenspan. And Duvid Norembursky took him away.

꿍

I want to think for a moment about the weight of judgment. Of who deserves to be judged, of who has the right to act as judge. I am not speaking here of public trials, of the court of public opinion, even of the judgments laid down by history. I am thinking of the judgments that reign in one's own heart, that prompt humility or hatred, that make one grateful for a kindness or make one ache in the night for revenge.

I feel free to judge the Germans for what they did during the war. And I find I even feel some satisfaction in being able to accuse them of their crimes.

In 1995, on the fiftieth anniversary of the war's end, I was invited to return to Lippstadt, where I had spent several months in another ammunitions factory we had been sent to from Auschwitz. Sometime in the 1980s, I think it was, a high school had been founded in Gütersloh, the neighboring town, for the city's very top students. The Anne Frank School, it was called. The students had been doing a good-works project—cleaning up a dilapidated old Jewish cemetery in Lippstadt—and as they were cutting back the weeds, clearing out the overgrowth, they had come upon a gravestone they didn't understand. The stone marked the grave of an infant who had died in 1945. This was odd, they thought, because the students had been taught that the last Jews had been evicted from the town by 1938; from 1938, they had been told, there were no Jews in Lippstadt. It was *judenrein*. So where had this child come from?

The students started researching their city's wartime history and eventually discovered that Jews and Russian prisoners of war had been made to work at an ammunitions factory that existed there. The gravestone marked the burial of a Jewish couple's baby who had died in 1945, just before the couple immigrated to Palestine. No one had ever told these students from the Anne Frank School—not their parents, not their grandparents—what had gone on in Lippstadt during the war, how prisoners were used as slaves to make weapons for the war. It had been erased from history. Until the gravestone of a Jewish baby brought that history to light.

The school decided to try to locate whomever they could who had worked in the factory. It took some doing, but they managed to find me and six or seven others. When they called me from Lippstadt inviting me to speak before the students during the fiftieth-anniversary commemoration, the school officials couldn't have been nicer. Would I like to bring my family along? Of course, we will pay. Your son is coming and eats only kosher food? We will get him a private chef to prepare whatever he would like. Please, remember that it's very cold and rainy here; don't forget to pack galoshes. Galoshes! Can you imagine? A German worrying about me that I shouldn't freeze or get my feet wet in the rain. I was dumbfounded.

Really, they were very kind, very solicitous.

When I spoke at the school, I wanted above all to make it clear that I wasn't accusing them—the students and teachers. The students were just children, maybe fifteen or sixteen years old; the teachers were perhaps thirty or forty. All of them, of course, had been born after the war. But I did want them to think about their parents and their grandparents: I wanted them to ask their families what they had done.

"Look," I said, "I didn't come here to accuse you of anything. All of you are young, and I will not judge you. But if you want to hear the truth and not just learn what is written in the histories of this town, then ask your parents directly. Ask your fathers and your grandfathers: What were you doing then? Every German wants to say that he was fighting the Russians, that he wasn't involved in this, he wasn't a part of what was done to the Jews. But how could that be? Some of your grandparents were murderers. And not only your grand-fathers—your grandmothers, too. The women could be the cruelest of all. Tell your grandparents that you want to know, that you are interested to know: What did they do, and what did they know during the war? Perhaps they will not tell you these things, but you should ask, because you should know who your grandparents were."

This was so satisfying to me, saying these things directly to these young people. It was so good to speak what was in my heart, to not hide, to not dissemble to them, even despite their overwhelming generosity to me and my family. It was a cleansing of some kind. Oddly perhaps, the young German students and teachers to whom I spoke seemed fully open to what I had to say, eager even to hear a survivor bring testi-mony to the history of their city, a history that the city itself had previously wanted to erase. That impressed me deeply, and still does.

But then, what about the Jews? Am I to judge my own people in the same way? Jews were the victims, not the criminals. Jack used to say that when history reflects on this time hun-dreds of years from now, it will be seen that, given everything, the Jews—as a whole, as a people—acted appropriately and generally with honor. That may well be true. But there were those among us who did unspeakable things to save them-selves, to save their families—or tried to. Is there any justifica-tion for that? I am thinking here not of history, but of my own life: Am I supposed to forgive someone who damns others to save himself?

I have forgiven some; in my heart I have. I feel no hatred for my cousin Elkanah Morgan, whom I will speak about, or for Chiel Friedman, who had been my uncle's friend. What these two men would do to me in the KL could easily have led to my death, but somehow I find that no enmity rises in me now at the mention of their names. But it is different with Duvid Norembursky. Though he was a Jew and thus surely in some way a victim, too, can I not raise my fist at his selfish cruelty? Can I not cry out at the horror of what he did? Of what he did to Heniek and the others? Of what he took from me?

Some years after the war, when Jack and I had settled in America, I did try to get some small justice, even to exact some small revenge against Norembursky and his wife. He didn't deserve the life he got. He had killed Heniek to get it. Or, perhaps better, perhaps more honest: He had caused Heniek to be killed. Was there to be no consequence? Was that murder to make no sound? To drop silently into the same abyss that every other murder had? How powerless it feels to sustain a blow and be unable to fight back. It feels like suffocating, like the natural back-and-forth of breath suddenly is no more. It feels like nothingness.

Heniek was gone, and I could not make him come back. Who was there to love me now? Who was there to shelter me?

And there was more to come.

The next day, I was arrested as well.

6

I WAS IN THE KITCHEN, BACK AT WORK, AS I HAD TO BE.
How could I be, I wonder? How could I sit again my on my
little stool and peel my daily quota of potatoes after Heniek
had been taken away? I had to do my work as if Heniek were
still with me, as if he might walk into the kitchen to check on
me, as if he still might meet me after my shift for a few private
moments. He would do none of those things, but still I had to
do my work. The factory, the kitchen—it was no different
from the ghetto: Terrible things happened, and no one could
stop to mourn. My life had ended, and yet still my life went
on. I don't know how that was possible.

I was in the kitchen, and my second cousin, Elkanah Morgan, came in. We called him Kunah. He had been a member
of the ghetto police, and he had come with Norembursky and
the others from the ghetto when they had replaced the factory
police just a few days earlier. I had known Kunah for years, of
course. He lived not far from my own home, and when I was

young, before the war, I was sometimes permitted to go to his family's apartment, not so much to visit him, but to spend some time with the wonderful thing he had built—a radio with earphones. This was a big deal in those days: Not everyone had a radio—we certainly didn't—and the earphones added wonder to the invention. Not often, but occasionally, and when I could, I would go and sit and listen with my cousins to Polish songs playing on Kunah's radio.

So when I saw Kunah enter the kitchen that day, I wasn't frightened at all. He was my cousin; he would never do anything to hurt me, to put me in danger. But then he came over to me and said, "Come with me." Simple. Just like that. "Come with me. I must take you because you are Greenspan."

Greenspan was Heniek's name, but mine was Drezner. There was no way to change my name legally when I got married. So although I was married to Heniek, I was still Mania Drezner, not Greenspan. Kunah knew this. But there was a girl named Greenspan—not related to Heniek—who was one of the girls Miller had chosen to work for him in the kuznia. She was several years older than I, and I knew that Miller had one day caught her kissing her boyfriend. I don't know if Miller punished her for that. But after Norembursky reported Miller for having committed Rassenschande, the police were required to arrest all the girls who had been involved, dozens of them. And Greenspan was one, and she was arrested. Still, why arrest me, too? I wasn't Greenspan, and I hadn't—thank God—worked in the kuznia.

Perhaps Kunah, like so many of the police, wanted to do more for the Germans than he had been asked. He had on his list of people to arrest one girl named Greenspan. But he would outdo the list: He would bring them two. He wouldn't listen to me.

"I am not Greenspan. You know this, Kunah. I am Drezner and have always been. I have nothing to do with this. Tell them you know that I didn't work in the kuznia. I have nothing to do with them."

But he was implacable. There was no convincing him. "Come," he said, "you have to go."

And I did. I always did as I was told. So my cousin took me out from the kitchen and led me to the gates of the KL compound, where twenty or so men and four or five women were nervously waiting. Kunah left me with these people, all of us silent and frightened and fidgeting in the cold. He walked away without saying anything to me—no explanation, no apology. Several other policemen were there, too. They told us to start walking and led us after maybe ten or fifteen minutes to a building none of us had ever been to before—the headquarters of the SS. This was where the Sicherheitsdienst was housed; this was where the Security Service tortured and executed suspected enemies of the Nazi regime; this, presumably, was where Duvid Norembursky had reported Miller's crimes. People taken to this place did not return. It was a place where people were killed.

The officers of the SD wore black uniforms, and everyone was petrified of them.

We were led through the main floor of the building and then down a flight of stairs. It was dark in the stairwell, and it was hard to see the steps as we descended. It began to seem that we were no longer in a building at all but rather going down under the earth. It smelled like the earth—a musty smell of moisture and dirt—a smell fit for animals.

At the bottom of the stairs, down a little ways, there was a room, though "room" is not really the right word for this place. It was like a dungeon dug out from the ground: The floor was just packed earth; there were no windows. There was a small, dim bulb hanging from the ceiling. It was the jail of the SD.

We were perhaps twenty-five people in this room, this dungeon. Eight or ten of the group were those rounded up in Miller's Rassenschande affair. The girl Greenspan was there—the one who had been caught kissing her boyfriend, the one on whose account Kunah had decided to arrest me.

Really, I was there because of her. I know this is not an entirely fair assessment: She had done nothing to cause my arrest—my arrest was through no fault of hers—but I was there because my cousin had brought me because I had the same name as hers. If she hadn't been chosen by Miller, Kunah would never have taken me. But in this girl Greenspan's mind, in her fear, in her desperation at what was surely about to ensue, the whole situation was the other way around.

"I'm here because of you!" she screamed. "You're the one who got me here! You got me arrested!"

This was crazy, of course.

"No one knows me as Greenspan. There are no papers, no documents. I am Mania Drezner, as I have always been. I have nothing to do with this," I kept protesting. But she wouldn't let go of it; she wouldn't listen to reason. She was just tormenting me with her accusations, unfounded, unreasonable, unending.

We were hours in that dungeon jail. It felt like years. Standing in the darkness, we could hear the screams from upstairs. Screams to make your bones sting. Screams that if there were a God, God would hear; if there were a God, God would make those screams stop.

No light. No food. No water. No rescue. No God.

The hours droned on.

They came in, the SS, the SD—I don't know who they were. They came in and took us out, one at a time. One by one. And between their visits to our dungeon, only screams.

No light. No food. No water.

No bathrooms.

People had to go. People needed to urinate. But there was nowhere to go in that earthen dungeon, and people knew they could be shot for soiling the floor. We were petrified that our waste might make a noticeable stench that would get us killed.

An absurd fear befitting an absurd place: We were going to be killed anyway in this place, whether we relieved ourselves or not. But how to avoid urinating in jail now became our focus, the searing focal point of our agony and apprehension.

What the men did! I didn't want to look; I didn't want to see their desperation. The men tied their penises. They tore off strips from their shirts, pulled pieces of string from their pockets, to tie tourniquets around their penises so the urine couldn't come out. They moaned in double distress, each man in his own private misery, trying to hold it in.

Then I, too, had to go. At first just a quiet pressure, a tingling almost, in my lower abdomen. I was used to this—we all were. During our shifts in the celownik, we weren't allowed to go to the bathroom whenever we needed to. At the end of the first six-hour shift, we were given fifteen minutes: If we needed to go, that's when we were allowed. But if we had to go earlier, then we just had to hold it—we had to wait until the end of the shift.

The body grows accustomed to its circumstance: I learned to hold it in, as we all did. The pressure would come, it would draw my attention, and then it would subside. At least for a time. When it returned, it would be more insistent, almost a bright spot, a pulsing knot of nerves deep inside my groin. But I learned to hold it in, in the factory, knowing that at some point, my six hours would be up.

It was different in the jail. The screaming upstairs, the shrieks of people I knew, of people who had been standing with me in that dankness just before. Me. I am next; they're going to take me next; now is when I am going to die. And the people moaning beside me, suffering in their own extremities of body and spirit, privately, miserably.

I thought I would burst. Not figuratively; this is not a way of speaking: I thought my bladder was going to rupture inside of me.

And then Zosia came to me. Zosia—an angel—the first of two that visited me that day.

Zosia Smuzik was a beautiful woman. Tall and strong, with pure white hair and high cheekbones. She didn't look Jewish; she looked Aryan, almost—and she spoke German flawlessly. I had known her a little from the kitchen, and we slept in the same barracks. I remember thinking how elegant she was, and confident, even in the extremity of our circumstances. Sometimes—where did she find the courage for this?—she would stand up to the Germans. Once, I heard her say to a German officer, "You want the Jews to work? Then you must feed them! They cannot work if they are weak from starvation!" Why was she not killed for these small acts of defiance?

Perhaps the Germans thought she was a Jewish sympathizer rather than a Jew. Perhaps that was why she wound up in the same jail as the rest of us; I don't know. Surely she hadn't been involved in the Rassenschande affair; she was a grown woman already, perhaps fifty or more. Were the Germans simply amused by her? By the absurdity of her belief that her insistence could make a difference?

I don't know. Perhaps it doesn't matter what she was to the Germans; I know what she was to us, to me.

Zosia saw that I was suffering, struggling to accomplish what physically was impossible—to keep myself from urinating. She came to me, removed the sweater she was wearing under her striped uniform, rolled it up in a tight ball, and held it out to me. She whispered, "Take off whatever you're wearing underneath and use this." It took me a moment to understand what she was suggesting, what she was offering. It was not as if she had sweaters to spare, as if she could throw this one away to be soiled by my urine and then easily slip into another to keep warm. Who knew how long we would be held in this jail? Who knew how long to shiver in the dark? She didn't know; it seems she didn't care. She saw my struggle; she wanted to give me ease; she wanted to give me her sweater.

I took it. I removed my underwear. I urinated into the warm ball of wool.

Then she drew us near, all of us. "Come," she said. "Come, my children; come to me. I want to tell you a story." Like a mother gathering her young, preparing her children for bed, Zosia called us to her. I couldn't be called a child—I was sixteen at the time, already a married woman—and everyone else in that jail was older than I. But Zosia had asked us to come; she had invited us into the embrace of her wisdom, and we drew ourselves to her as to the warmth and light of a household hearth.

"My children," she said, "we are going to die here. This is true. But when we are shot in this horrible place, we will go straight up to Heaven. And you will see when you come up, you will see that the angels will be there, waiting for us."

She was speaking to grown people, to men and women who hadn't heard bedtime stories in decades, to men and women not given to fantasies of Heaven and angels. And yet. And yet. We listened, hungry, starving for her words.

"You will see, my children, that there will be long tables with white tablecloths. And all the tables will be piled high with foods of every sort you can imagine—oranges and pineapples and meats and cheese and bread still warm from the fire. And the angels will be happy for us, happy to see us there with them, and they will dance around us and cheer our arrival into their midst."

This was bliss; this was sublime—to lose ourselves for some moments, some minutes, in the midst of that awful place. We listened to her speak, and for those minutes, I was no longer in that jail, no longer clutched by fear. What a gift she gave us! What a godsend. I didn't care if what she said was foolishness; in those moments, it was real to me, and I was willing for her words to be more real, more true, than the crushing truth I saw around me. Her vision offered me light and hope and freedom, and I was more than ready to make her vision mine. I never forgot the feeling of those few moments of relief. It was a foretaste of Heaven, whatever Heaven might be.

Zosia and me in the 1960s

Zosia survived her time in the SD jail, one of the very few who did. She survived the war, as well. We found each other, years later. She was living in Israel, in a small town called Pardes Hannah. She had aged, of course, since the last time I had seen her, but she still had that self-possessed elegance I so admired. Jack and I would visit her whenever we traveled to Israel, and we would always bring small packages of food with us, filling them with canned tuna and coffee and jams—anything we thought might have been hard to find in Israel in those days. I always wanted to be giving Zosia something—even little things. She had given me so much.

Once during a visit, I asked what possessed her that day in the jail, what had brought to mind the idea of telling us this story about Heaven and angels and a feast we couldn't possibly enjoy. She told me then about a movie she had seen, a Polish movie, I think, in which a man was jailed for some terrible crime and was awaiting execution. The man was suffering from fear, awaiting his end. His jailer, noticing his agony, took pity on him and looked around for someone to visit him, to talk with him, to ease his sense of doom. But search as he might, the jailer was unable to find anyone who would agree to visit this criminal, until he found a prostitute, a woman already shamed, already beaten down by the world, and unable to hold herself in higher regard than a convict. This woman came to the jail and sat with the man for some time. She told him a story, of Heaven and angels and tables overflowing with food. And he sat and listened to her, rapt in her imaginings, and for that time, his heart was eased, his fears diminished. Zosia had thought of this movie when we were huddled together in that jail. Though we were not criminals, though she was not a prostitute, we were all there, rejected by the world, with no one to offer us comfort in what we were sure would be—and what for many of us was— our final hours. So Zosia thought to comfort us with the story line of a movie she had seen, and her little plan worked. For me, I can say, it worked.

က

But, then, truly, for how long could it work? Like waking from a dream, like opening my eyes again from the silken warmth of a midnight sleep into the air of a frigid room in winter, we roused ourselves from Zosia's reverie and returned again to the desolation of our jail. Still we were there below the SD headquarters. There was still the endless wait for a soldier to come and call our names, still the screams, still the desperation.

And still Greenspan, tormenting me. "What am I doing here? What have you done to me? It is because of you. I am here because of you."

It was unbearable. I thought I could take no more.

Then I heard someone calling to me in the dim light. "Mania, I know who you are. I know you are not Greenspan."

A small man—his name was Katz. I didn't know who he was, but he apparently knew me. He was an informer, I later found out, and he had been arrested and brought to the jail because the Germans didn't trust their informers: The Germans used them, gave them protection for a time, and then executed them, along with everyone else.

Katz said to me, "I want to make you a promise. If they will take me first, I will tell them who you are. I will tell them that you are not Greenspan, and that you never worked in the kuznia. I will tell them that you are here only because of a name association. If they will take me first, I promise I will let them know."

Why this gift? Why this kindness out of nowhere? I had no explanation, no more than I had for Zosia's grace or Greenspan's crazed accusation or Kunah's adamant insistence that he take me away. Perhaps before he died, Katz wanted to expiate his own sins. Had he informed on Jews? On his friends? Had he sent people to death? I don't know what prompted him to offer me this gift, without any hope of possible recompense. And I was never able to ask him, because soon the soldiers came and called his name. They took him out. We heard the screams. I never saw him again.

They came for me maybe fifteen minutes later. I didn't imagine that Katz's efforts could have done any good. What was now ahead of me? A beating? A shot to the head? Would the prisoners now huddle together listening to my screams as I was interrogated by the SD? What could I possibly tell them? I had nothing to say. I didn't know anything. I was so terribly afraid of being beaten.

I was led by two soldiers, each one gripping me tightly by the arm. I cannot express what I felt walking up those stairs, walking down the passageway to the interrogation room. I couldn't see clearly where I was going. I was numb; I could barely breathe. I didn't have a trace of hope.

The soldiers took me into a small room. It smelled dusty, but sharp, too, as if metal had recently been polished. There was a table and a chair and two German officers, one by the table, the other by the door. I stood still, trying to keep upright, trying not to let on how close I was to collapse. The man by the table stared at me for a moment, then walked calmly to me; he opened his gloved hand and without a word struck me hard across the face. Smack. Then again and again, the hard, smooth leather raising welts on my cheeks.

I had never been hit before. The pain was sharp, like the smell of the room, bright almost—the sting concentrating in my face but somehow also radiating through my body. I was shocked by it. I can't say caught off guard, because I knew the blow was coming, but I was shocked by the pain itself, the first flash and then the searing throbs, a pulsing in my body in rhythm with my racing heart.

I tried hard not to cry. I stood there, trying to steady my breath, trying simply to look ahead, to stare at nothing.

The officer brought his face close to mine. I could feel his breath against my cheek. "You must tell no one about this place. You were never here and you never saw anything and you never heard anything. Do you understand this? Do you understand?"

Still looking ahead, away from him, I nodded, yes, yes, I understand.

"You can go back to the kitchen," he said, "but you will say nothing. We will know if you do. We have people who will know, and they will tell. If we hear that you have spoken about this place, we will bring you back here and you will never get out."

And then he nodded to the man at the door, and two soldiers came in to take me out. They walked me through the hall and out the front door and to the gate of the compound, where I was met by two of the Jewish police.

With that, simply, inexplicably, I was returned from the dead.

Of the twenty or so people in that basement jail, only three or four made it out alive. I did, and Zosia, too, and a couple of others I heard about later. The rest were killed. Katz was killed, having saved my life. The girl Greenspan, who was said to be pregnant at the time, was beaten so badly that all her teeth were knocked out, before she, too, was killed.

When I got back to the compound, I saw scores of people waiting behind the barbed-wire fence, looking out, watching for my return. They must have heard that someone was going to be released from the place from which no one ever returned. A miracle was to happen, and people wanted to see. So there

MILLIE WERBER AND EVE KELLER

they were, dozens and dozens of them, people I knew and people I didn't know, standing at the gates, watching me.

I didn't want to see anyone. I knew I was not allowed to speak to anyone. I walked into the compound and went silently to my barracks. Mima was there and greeted me calmly and with affection. She asked, but I wouldn't say anything about what had happened—not then, and not for years after. The Germans had frightened me so, telling me not to tell. That order embedded itself so deeply in me that I didn't—really, I couldn't—tell. Eventually, only long after the war was over, I told Jack, but only a very little, only the outlines.

This was the second time my life had been saved by a stranger. Unprompted, unrequited, first Zwirek and now Katz had offered up on my behalf acts of real goodness, of human, selfless good-heartedness. But I cannot say that the two were the same for me. I was alive, but, truly, so what? I was alive, but Heniek, I had to assume, was dead. I was alive, but to what end? To build what future? With whom?

Yes, I was relieved to have been saved. I do not wish to diminish the weight of this. But I was broken, too.

7

Somehow Duvid Norembursky had managed to get Polish papers—papers that identified him and his family as Polish rather than Jewish. He kept them as a kind of insurance policy, a backup plan in the event that his status as a member of the Jewish police might one day no longer protect him. When, soon after he arrived in the Konzentrationslager, Miller's two policemen came from the kuznia looking for him, Norembursky realized that this day had come. Miller, it turned out, was still in power; the girls whom he had abused in the kuznia had been punished—most had been killed—but Miller had managed to avert punishment for himself. Now, it seemed, he was out for revenge; he was looking to get back at the one who had reported him for committing Rassenschande. Norembursky had planned to protect himself by getting into the factory compound. Suddenly, he saw that everything was burning under his feet; the place wasn't safe for him at all.

The papers he had stashed away were for himself, his wife, his paternal aunt and uncle and their little girl, his cousin, who was perhaps eight or nine years old. He had hoped to save others besides himself. I need to remember this, because it helps me remember that there was once some humanity to the man. He didn't start out heartless.

I don't know if that makes it better or worse.

When he heard that the police from the kuznia had come looking for him, Norembursky knew he had to find a way out of the KL. To save himself, he was willing to abandon everything—his family, his humanity, too. For every one who escapes, twenty will be killed: Norembursky knew this; we all did.

He took his wife and ran.

The other three whom he had papers for, who were supposed to go with him—the aunt, uncle, and their child—they ran, too, but only after Norembursky and his wife had already left, and by then it was too late.

Norembursky and his wife escaped. I don't know the details: how they managed to escape the KL, where they hid—if they did—or whether they were easily able to pass as Poles. I know that eventually they made it to America, and I know they raised a family under changed names. I do not know about any perils they may have encountered on their journey. I do not know if they were ever afraid. I do not know if they ever suffered from nightmares for what they did. I just know that they escaped. I know what happened afterward.

They escaped. Damn them! They escaped.

The police found Norembursky's aunt, uncle, and little cousin, and they were brought back to the KL the next day.

Then the killing began.

We were made to come out to the yard—I was working my shift in the kitchen at the time. We were brought out into the fresh air, pressing together against the inevitability of what we knew was about to happen. We were made to watch.

The soldiers had with them the three who had been caught, and lined them up against a wall. The little girl was holding her mother's hand. The Germans raised their guns; someone yelled an order; they fired. Three bodies fell to the ground—a man, a woman, a child.

But the Germans needed more. Someone must have told them about Norembursky's wife's family; they were in the KL, too. So Norembursky's mother-in-law, brother-in-law, and nephew, a young boy who, I remember, was on crutches for some reason—they were found and brought to the yard. The Germans then added seventeen more, people they grabbed out of the barracks for no reason we could figure, people, as far as we knew, wholly unconnected to Norembursky or his wife. Just people, just Jews. But now there were twenty; beyond the three killed for trying to escape, there were now twenty gathered in the yard to be executed because of Norembursky and his wife.

I have tried, all these years, to understand the choices Norembursky and his wife made. They knew that others would be killed if they managed to get away. (And truly, there should have been forty, not twenty, according to the Germans' threat.) Did this not matter to them? When Norembursky feared for his own life, when he learned that Miller was after him and that his position as a policeman would offer him no protection, in the immediacy of that moment did he think at all? Did he reason like a man, weighing what his escape would mean? Or did he act then only in accordance with some older, baser nature?

If you act as a beast in a moment when it matters, is it possible ever to become a man again? But then, I do not think that even beasts do this—betray a parent to save their own skin.

I heard a story once, a terrible story from Warsaw. A Jewish policeman was ordered to round up some number of fellow Jews. He did his job, but for some reason, when he was finished with the roundup, he was one man short. He needed to make up the number; otherwise, he himself would be killed. So the man went to his father and asked if he would go. Would he, the father, allow his son to take him to the Germans so that his own life—the son's life—might be saved?

I try to imagine this. I try to envision the scene:

"Father, I have come to ask you for something."

"Yes, my son. What do you need?"

"Father, I need one more man to give to the Germans. If I do not bring them one more man, they will kill me. You are old, Father, and I am young. I am asking you, Father, will you go for me?"

How does the mouth form this question? Does the man look in his father's eyes when he asks this? Or does he turn his head away, torn between damnable desire and ferocious shame? And what is in the father's heart when he responds? What is in this father's heart when he says yes, when he agrees to go, when he submits to death so his son might live?

How is it possible for one to ask this of another human being? How does one ask this of a father?

Norembursky, of course, didn't even ask. He ran with his wife, knowing others would pay for their freedom.

How could they ever be free after that?

Those who died because of Norembursky did not perform an act of silent martyrdom. No one here went willingly to their death.

The soldier dragged Norembursky's mother-in-law from the barracks. Frenzied with fear, she was crying hysterically, screaming through her tears. She called out to us gathered to watch her execution.

"If any of you survives," she shouted, "if any of you makes it out of here, you must find my daughter and tell her she will never be alone. The souls of her mother and her family will haunt her always; they will swirl around her and never let her be. This is my curse!"

That is how she died, cursing her daughter, begging us to tell her, should we ever find her, that her mother died with this curse on her lips.

These words—word for word—they have stayed with me exactly; I can recite them today just as I heard them, many decades ago.

Jack used to say that we cannot condemn what the Jews did during the war. The fear of dying was so great, how can we judge?

I don't know. I don't know.

I think about my own mother.

I missed my mother so desperately when I was at the factory. I didn't know if I would see her again, and I so longed for her love. A daughter needs her mother's love. Does a mother not need her daughter's love as well? A daughter's devotion? Do we not owe our mothers some obligation, a life lived in some conscious gratitude for the life that they gave to us? Our mothers made us. How can a daughter knowingly cause her mother pain?

Soon after we were liberated and came into the town of Kaunitz, an American soldier saw that I was hungry and that I owned only the frayed dress and coat I had been given when we left Auschwitz. The American soldier took me into a small house so I could find what I needed, so I could take whatever I wanted for food, for clothes. The Germans had lost the war; the Americans had won, and now the victors could take whatever they chose. This American man was trying to extend a kindness to me. He wasn't out to terrorize anyone; he wasn't out to cause any pain. He simply thought I needed clothes. But when we entered this house, the woman who lived there was overcome with fright—her hands were shaking, her eyes wide; she kept taking steps backward to move herself farther away from this foreign man in army uniform.

I could have had anything I wanted from that house: food, clothes, shoes—whatever I needed or desired, I could have taken. But when I saw that German lady cowering in such fear, all I could see was my mother, a vision of my mother as the Germans barged their way into her tiny room in the ghetto when they came to send her to Treblinka, my mother trembling and hopeless and miserable, knowing she was vanquished, knowing she was helpless in her enemies' hands. I saw my mother in this German lady's fear, and I ran. I couldn't take anything from her; I couldn't be the cause of her terror.

Did Norembursky's wife have no misgivings about the terror she caused her mother? Did she run envisioning her mother's despair?

Oh my daughter! What have you done to me?

When Norembursky and his wife fled, did they think of their families at all? That first night, did nightmares of gunshots wake them from their sleep? Norembursky and his wife escaped, and in escaping, they consigned twenty others to death. They bought their lives—first in coming to the factory and then in escaping from it—they bought their own lives with the lives of others. They paid for their survival in currency that wasn't theirs to give. Heniek and twelve other policemen along with their families were taken away so that Norembursky and his fellows could move to the factory; now twenty others were executed because Norembursky and his wife escaped.

All these lives, all this blood, is on them.

ಞಞ

Norembursky and his wife survived the war, and I found them, several years later, after we had all immigrated to America. Jack and I were living, as squatters essentially, in a mostly abandoned building on Lewis Street, on the Lower East Side in New York. My father had found work in the garment district, and one day, he came by our apartment and told me that he had seen Norembursky's wife working in the garment district, too, but now living under an assumed name. This outraged me—not just that Norembursky had managed to survive, but that he and his wife were living in New York with new identities. Norembursky was living as if he could erase his past and all the things he was accountable for. In a world of infinite injustice, this struck me as intolerable.

There was no explanation for who survived and who perished—I knew this even then, just as I know it now. I survived by luck and happenstance and several times by the unprompted kindness of strangers. Zwirek had saved my life; Katz had saved my life. Why did the SD let me leave that jail? What could it have mattered to them, even if they knew, even if they were convinced that I was not the Greenspan they were looking for? So what? The Germans killed indiscriminately; they never waited for just cause to commit murder. So why did they let me go?

I cannot fathom a reason for my survival. I was innocent; I survived. These are two truths, but they are separate truths; no logical chain of thought connects them. One cannot draw a line that gets you from how you lived to whether you died. Some innocents lived; many innocents—hundreds, thousands . . . millions of innocents—died. And the guilty, too. It is no different for them. Some were killed, yes—even by Jews—as Tannenbaum was beaten to death by Jews when he was taken with the rest of us to Auschwitz. But being guilty didn't mean that you would die. I knew this then; I know this now. And yet. It was, despite this, an outrage to me that Duvid Norembursky was alive and living under an assumed name. In a world of infinite injustice—truly, I did understand that I wasn't going to find justice for what had happened—still, I could not let this be.

I went to the Office of Immigration. I was just nineteen at the time. I spoke almost no English; I didn't know how to talk with people in offices, people who sat behind desks with an air of authority. I wasn't one to demand things, to look people in the eye. Still, I went to the Office of Immigration to make a protest, to let them know that there was someone living in New York under a false identity, someone who had committed crimes and must now be called to account. "His real name is Duvid Norembursky," I said, "and he has the death of many Jews on his hands. He doesn't belong here; he has no right to live here. He's pretending to be someone he's not."

What proof did I have? they wanted to know. How could I demonstrate that he was not who he claimed to be? For crimes committed in Poland, in Germany, they could do nothing; they had no jurisdiction over things that happened in other countries. But they could pursue the false identity, if I could prove that this man was not who he said he was.

How could I do that? Not that I didn't want to, but what proof did I have? I knew who he was; I knew what he had done. But I had no way to prove it, however much I wanted to.

Still, word must have reached them that I was trying to have them found, hoping to get them deported, because one day, Norembursky's wife showed up at my door on Lewis Street. She pleaded with me, begged me to let them be, to leave them alone to their new lives in America. The war is over, she said; it's all in the past now. Just let us be. Please, please—you must let us be.

I knew I would not be able to succeed in getting them in trouble with the authorities. But I could do one thing: I could tell Norembursky's wife what her mother had said as she went to her death. And I did. I told her. Your mother died cursing you, spitting your name in agony. I will never let you be, she said, my soul will haunt you, will swirl around you and never let you find peace.

I told her this, and—let me say it, because however horrible, however cruel, it is true—I was glad to do it; I was glad to give her this pain. It gave me some satisfaction to know that she would now have to face the full weight of what she had done. She would live with the certain knowledge that, in effect, she had killed her own mother, that her mother knew this, and that her mother had cursed her for it. And—I am trying to be honest here; I am trying to say honestly what I feel—I do not regret doing this, even now, even all these years later. Still, the world is one of infinite injustice—Heniek is still dead, the mother is still dead, the brother, the nephew, and all the others, too—but I was able to say just a little so that those deaths were not without consequence, not without a sound.

The horror you cause shall cause horror to you.

8

THE WORST PART WAS THE RATS. I WAS PETRIFIED THAT they were going to eat my eyes.

Several days after the Noremburskys' escape, a man I knew came into the barracks to give me some news. Szlamek Horowitz was his name, and he worked as a *Schreiber*—a secretary of some kind—in the administrative office of the Konzentrationslager. I didn't know him well, but sometimes we would chat for a moment or two when he came to the barracks to check on his mother. When he approached me that day in the barracks, I thought perhaps he simply was stopping by to say hello. But, no, it was something else.

Not long before this, soon after the KL had been established, our factory, which made munitions, was joined to an adjacent one, which made baskets. The two factories had previously worked as separate entities, with separate administrations, separate barracks, and separate kitchens, but now their living quarters were enclosed in the same compound, behind the same barbed wire. Szlamek told me that the Germans had decided that the two kitchens were to be merged and that all those who worked in my kitchen—the butchers, the vegetable peelers, and the two or three men who managed the place—were now considered superfluous. Tomorrow morning, there would be an oblava: We were all to be rounded up and taken away.

An oblava. And I was to be a part of it. This time, there would be no confusion about my name. They knew who worked in the kitchen. I was particularly known, because Heniek had somehow made special arrangements to get me there. I was going to be taken away. From the kitchen, from the barracks, from Mima and Feter, from anything I had known. And taken where? To be again alone, exposed, unprotected. A meager slip of a girl, buffeted by winds.

Is it possible ever to accustom oneself to a daily threat of death? It had been days only—maybe two, maybe three, certainly not six or seven—since I had been taken to the jail. Everything at once—all that treachery and death and trembling fear. How does anyone absorb that? I was so very young, and everything about me was so huge in its proportions. I was married and then my husband was taken from me; I was to die in a hellish jail, and then I was saved; and now again—just minutes later, it felt like—not even before I could learn again to breathe, I was to be brought to the threshold of death. Again. How is it possible for a life to be composed of crisis upon crisis with no room in between? How is it possible to maintain one's balance in such a dizzying world?

Szlamek said to me, "Look here: Your name is on this list of workers who will be liquidated. I will do what I can to erase your name, but you mustn't count on me. I don't know what I can do. It may not be enough. You must try to do something for yourself. Take off this dress; put on whatever you have from home. Maybe you can escape."

What? Escape? How? Where? Where could I go? I could never escape, especially not after what had happened with Norembursky. What could I do? All of us were required to go to our appointed places of work every morning; no one was allowed to stay back in the barracks. But once I got to the kitchen, Szlamek said, I would be taken with everyone else.

I ran to find Mima and Feter. What should I do? Szlamek Horowitz, the Schreiber from the office—you know him, yes? He said he would try, but I mustn't rely on him, he said; I must figure something out on my own.

That night is an utter blank to me. Did I sleep? I wonder. Did I pray? Perhaps I sneaked into Mima's bunk and buried myself in her arms; perhaps she tried to comfort me, to assure me that I would be safe. How she could have mouthed these words, I don't know; I can't imagine I would have believed them.

In the morning, I stayed behind in the barracks when everyone else went out to work. It would be trouble if I got caught dawdling in the morning routine, but I knew it would be worse if I left for the kitchen. I couldn't stay where I was, yet there was nowhere I could go.

Mima and Feter came into the barracks.

I could hear the Germans in the yard, starting to call out the names of the workers from the kitchen.

Feter turned to me: "You must hide. We have to hide you."

The barracks we were made to sleep in were fairly shoddy, built by forced labor to house the several thousand people who worked in and for the factory. The structures had no foundation under them and no cement or concrete flooring. Wooden planks had just been laid onto the ground, set down side by side on the packed dirt, and nailed roughly together.

Feter went over to the side of the barracks, and with a single, strong heave, he ripped up the floorboard underneath one of the bunks. "Here," he said. "Quickly. Get in here. Come quickly."

He was holding up the floorboard, motioning for me to get in.

I did as I was told. I went over to where he was standing; he grabbed me and pushed me down toward the small space of ground exposed by the torn-up floorboard. There was barely enough space for me to fit—twelve inches, maybe, between the packed dirt underneath the building and the wooden floor built on top. I shimmied myself in, using my hands to jostle my body into place. I lay flat against the cold ground, looking up at my uncle, who was holding the floorboard above me.

"Maniusia," he said. "You must not move. You must not make a sound."

I was terrified. It was not in my nature, hiding like this, doing anything that was against the rules. I wasn't brave; I wasn't one to take risks. I did as I was told, never trying to put myself forward, never strategizing about how to make my chances of survival better. It's not that I didn't want to survive; it's that I wasn't built to take risks, to push my way forward. I was always hiding, I suppose, in some way—hiding in the crowd, hiding to escape notice. But hiding like this— hiding beneath a building when I was supposed to be showing up for kitchen duty—this just wasn't like me. I never would have hidden on my own; I never would have even thought to do it, let alone figure out where.

Feter lowered the floorboard over my head. I could hear him push it into place with his foot and then walk away.

I was alone.

It was completely dark, and the place smelled musty and stale and damp. I had to be still; I had to be quiet, but I was petrified and I could hear my heart hammering in my chest.

And then I heard the scratching. Little scraping noises all around me. Little feet, tiny feet scampering in the dirt. Lots of them. Rats. Rats, scurrying all around—beside me, along my legs, up onto my torso. They climbed on my face. I saw them, looking into my eyes, their noses twitching, their whiskers against my cheeks, their tails back and forth against my neck. My God! It was horrible, horrifying.

I squeezed my eyes tight; I wanted to shield my face with my hands, but I was wedged in too tightly—I couldn't bring my hands up from my sides. I wanted to shield my eyes so the rats wouldn't get at them. I thought they wanted to eat my eyes.

I was hidden from the Germans, but utterly exposed to the rats. I tried to compress myself as compactly as I could: legs forced against each other, arms tight against my sides, hands squeezed hard into fists. I pressed my lips together, I screwed up my eyes. I was a single, rigid entity, a board lying stiff under the boards. I tried desperately not to move; I tried barely to breathe. Still they came—over my face, over my eyes, into my hair.

I lay there forever, resisting every urge to thrash about. Two hours it maybe was, or maybe ten minutes—forever.

Then came a noise from outside. Someone had entered the barracks. I heard the hard thudding of someone walking with determination, someone intent and angry. A few steps, then pause, then a few steps more.

"Where are you? I know you're here!"

It was Chiel Friedman, the Jewish policeman in charge of the KL. I had had no dealings with him personally, but I had often heard him barking his orders to us—to go here or line up there or to hurry along. His coarse, throaty voice was unmistakable—like sandpaper on stone—and there was no mistaking it now. He knew that I was one of the kitchen workers, because Heniek had had to go through him to get me transferred from the celownik to the kitchen. He had come to the barracks knowing I must be there—there was nowhere else I could be.

"Come out from your hiding! You know I will find you!"

His voice was scratchy but driven, a knife cutting into the quiet where I lay. The rats startled at his rough call and seemed to pause for a moment in their scurrying.

Don't move; don't move, I told myself, squeezing myself even tighter, contracting myself inward, my body tense, vibrating against its own pressure.

I heard his footsteps, the dull creak of the wooden boards as he walked around the floor.

Oh God! Oh God! Please don't find me. Please don't look for me here.

The rats were swarming again, crawling over me as if I were part of the ground, as if I were a piece of the earth. I willed myself not to move.

He was marching now, up and down the aisles of the barracks. He started to scream, furious that he hadn't found me. "You whore! I know you are in this barracks! I'm going to find you, Heniek's little whore!"

Was it not enough that he was hunting me down? Did he have to debase me as well? Dirty me with the stink of his slur? I wanted to scream back at him: "Heniek's wife, you animal! His wife, not his whore!"

It was some poison in Friedman, some venom in his blood that he was spewing out at me. I wanted it off. As much as I wanted the rats off, I wanted that word off me. It was an outrage I didn't deserve.

Friedman looked for me everywhere, but somehow he didn't think to look where I was. Somehow he didn't look under the floorboards, where a young girl lay trembling in fear and fury under a coat of rats.

He strode out of the building.

Feter must have been waiting outside, because he returned to the barracks almost immediately and ran to lift the floor above my head. The rats fled with the sudden light, and I pulled myself up into the air. The oblava was over.

The Germans seemed not to care. Now that the workers from the other kitchen took over the work in ours, I was given a job back in the munitions factory, lifting and cutting long and heavy steel bars. The job was too hard for me—I was too small to be able to maneuver the bars effectively—and somehow, though I don't remember how, I was able to use the money Heniek had given me to get transferred to another part of the factory—it was called the montage—where I put together some of the pieces that made up revolvers. It seemed not to matter to the Germans that I had escaped the oblava. After that one day, they didn't send anyone to come looking for me.

But it mattered to Chiel Friedman. He resented it, resented that I had managed to elude him. I think he had wanted to show the Germans how good he was at his policing job, to show them that he could ferret out the young girl who tried to avoid capture. So it angered him that he was unable to do this, that a mere girl had won. He never said anything to me about it, but whenever I saw him after that in the KL compound, he would stare at me with an intensity that frightened me, a ferocity that said, "I know who you are. I know how to harm you." I would look away, pretending not to have seen him, not to have noticed the menace in his eyes.

Friedman was the one who had slapped my uncle and had told him that he was to be called "Commander," to distinguish himself from everyone else. He was the one to whom my uncle would say, when they were liberated together from Dachau, "For me the war has ended, but for you it has just begun."

ןיני

So it was for Friedman. Nobody wanted to have anything to do with him after the war. He went to Garmisch-Partenkirchen along with the many other Radomers, but people didn't want to know him. People had so many things against him, he was afraid even to leave his house.

Eventually—and reluctantly—he married a woman he thought beneath him. Like most of the Jewish police, Friedman had his matura. He was intelligent, educated; he came from a family rich enough to send him to school. Before the war, he would have been considered a good catch. But this woman he married was *prost*—common, vulgar; she came from a lowly family, barely more than peasants. She was strongly built and burly, like someone made for physical labor. People said she looked like a cow. In Poland, before the war, she might have been his maid.

Friedman married her—Chava was her name—but only because he saw that he was a lost man, that he had no chance in Germany. I think he believed that at some point, the Jews might even kill him. Chava had family in Canada, and she proposed to him that if he married her, he could go to Canada with her and start over, away from the Radomers who reviled him. He was reluctant, but he was desperate: Chava offered a way out.

Here is the amazing part. When he married Chava, this woman he didn't love, this woman he believed was so much beneath him, he actually invited Jack and me to the wedding. Jack, it turned out, was a cousin of his, and Friedman had no other family to invite.

Had Friedman forgotten what he had done to me? How he had searched for me and cursed me as the rats ran over my face?

We declined the invitation.

Years later, he came to my house. It was probably the 1970s by then. Jack and I had become close to his sister, Luba, and once, when she was visiting from Israel, she asked if her brother could meet her at our house in New York. Luba had not seen him at all in the decades since the war. She never talked about him with us, and we never asked her what she knew about the things he had done. I supposed she asked us to meet him in our house because she wanted to see him somewhere where their own conversation might be moderated by others around. Chiel (as we called him by then) flew in from Toronto, and we offered to pick him up from the airport and bring him over for a couple of hours so he and Luba could talk. Mima and Feter were living next to us at that time in Jackson Heights, and I kept from them the news that Chiel was coming—Feter would never have permitted it; he never would have sanctioned Chiel's stepping into my house.

I have to say, even after everything, I felt sorry for him: He suffered so much—from fear, maybe, or from guilt, I don't know. When Jack and I met him at the airport, I could see that he was looking around, checking all about him to see if anyone was out to get him. He was in New York, a city of millions, and yet he was afraid that some Radomer might be lurking somewhere in Idyllwild Airport, waiting in a corner to pounce on him.

He came to the house, sat in my living room, and spent two hours complaining. How he was being so badly mistreated by the Radomers, how people were exaggerating the things he had done, telling lies about his past. What had he ever done that was so bad? That deserved such treatment? And who, after the war, he wanted to know, had done so much for someone else?

It was true, that part. Chiel had been married before the war—his wife and son both died in Auschwitz—and this woman, Chiel's first wife, had a brother who had paid a Polish family to take in his young daughter during the war. But the father, Chiel's brother-in-law, didn't survive, and after Chiel came to Canada, he spent a lot of effort—and I'm sure a lot of money—tracking down this girl in Poland. At first, the little girl didn't want to go with him—she had been raised Catholic by people she thought of as her parents—but she did eventually agree to go, provided that Chiel would promise to take care of her Polish family. He sent a sewing machine to the little girl's "sister," and he sent monthly packages to her "parents."

Chiel took in his brother-in-law's daughter and raised her as his own. Yes, this is true. But why did he do this thing? He claimed it was proof of his goodness, that only a good man would have gone to such trouble for a child not his own. But I think he did it for himself, to make himself feel better about whatever he had done during the war. I don't even think he was trying to atone, because that would have meant coming to terms with his past; that would have required some inner reckoning, some recognition that he had done wrong during the war. I don't think Chiel was ever capable of that kind of self-reflection or self-knowledge. His habit was to make excuses for himself: He had been afraid for his life; he had wanted to protect his wife and his son. Of course, he never said these things—not to me, not to Jack. I don't think he would have said them to anyone. But I believe he said them to himself, at night, perhaps, when maybe it would have been hard to fall asleep. Then maybe he would remind himself, again and again, that he had raised his niece as his own, which surely proved that he was a good man, after all. Wrapping himself in half-truths, trying to bring comfort to his quiet hours, to bring calm to his conscience at night.

All of us, I suppose, tell ourselves stories about our lives, stories that make it easier to live with ourselves and the choices we have made. If you tell yourself a story long enough and often enough, you might in fact come to believe it: "I didn't have a choice. I was only trying to protect my family. And look, I raised this child." You might even come to substitute the good version of yourself for the truer but more insidious one. But I don't believe that in a sane mind, in a sane man, that substitution can ever be complete; some part of you must always know the cruelty at your core. And that must be hell.

Though I could never soften to Chiel, I believe I eventually forgave him. It was so clear to me that he was living in a jail after the war. That jail was built by the Radomers, to be sure, but all his self-justifications, all his storytelling—these were part of his jail, too. He wanted to turn his back on the truth of his past in order to find some peace for himself in the present. To the day he died, I don't think he found it.

9

I REMEMBER ALMOST NOTHING ABOUT MY LAST FIVE OR SIX months in the KL at Radom. After the ruin of winter, the earthquakes and aftershocks, what was left? Darkness, maybe; a sense of nothingness. My life had exploded in the tumult of those days, though surely I shouldn't here be using terms drawn from the natural world to describe them. These weren't natural disasters, not natural events even in the mystifying course of human history. Those several weeks during the winter of 1943–1944 were, for me at least, an eruption of the worst humankind was capable of; they tore from me any sense I may have had that life was for living, that life held in store riches and promise and pleasure. Having lost Heniek—and because of a Jew, no less—I felt I had lost everything. It felt almost an affliction to live, an emptiness to be endured.

Still, I must remember Zosia; I must remember Katz. And Szlamek, too, and Feter, who told me where to hide. I must remember their simple goodness when my own life was imperiled, for their goodness was true, too, flickering in the dark.

༼ༀༀ༽

In the late spring and summer of 1944, rumors began circulating that the Russians were advancing from the east. A man who worked with us in the factory but somehow had connections outside it—maybe he knew a Pole still living a relatively normal life in Radom—fed us information. He said the Americans had landed in France and that he was certain they would break through Germany's forces in Western Europe. The Russians, he told us, were already in Poland, now just thirty kilometers from Radom.

We didn't dare to hope, but this was joyous news. We thought the Russians would be our saviors. We prayed for their advance, for their imminent arrival to liberate us. The Germans were scared; they wanted out.

They decided to empty the camp.

It was the end of July, almost exactly two years since I had begun working at the factory. Two thousand men and nearly five hundred women were all now to be taken out, made to leave, made to go . . . where? We didn't know. We knew only that we had to leave Radom. We were going to be made to walk.

Szlamek found me and advised me, again, to put on my civilian clothes under my striped uniform. He must have been still thinking of escape; he must have been thinking that the walk—wherever we were walking—would offer opportunities to run.

I put on what I had—a sweater, I remember, maybe a blouse. We collected whatever we still had from the ghetto and could secretly carry. Szlamek's mother wore a pocketed belt under her dress; I didn't know then what she kept in it. Before she moved to the factory, Mima had opened a hollow space in the heel of one of her shoes; she then sealed in it a small ring of hers. I had the little pocket sewn into my panties; to the two gold wedding bands, I now added my only other treasure—the picture of me and Heniek.

Then we left. Every Jew who was still in Radom—the factory workers, those who had worked in the shops taken over by the Germans, the informers, the police—every Jew was gathered together to begin a march to we-didn't-know-where.

In my whole life, I had been outside of Radom only once, when Mama brought me along with her to a spa in Busko-Zdrój, where she was treated for rheumatism. Other than that—and my little journey to Jedlińsk—everything else was Radom, the city of my family for generations. I remember in the ghetto seeing my grandfather cry for fear of a deportation that would keep him from having a proper Jewish burial in Radom. I think perhaps even more than dying, he feared not having his bones rest in Radom's Jewish cemetery.

The factory, too, and the whole complex of the KL—they were known, familiar worlds by this time as well. Even the dangers were known—the factory machinery, the guards with their guns, the roundups, and the hunger and the disease and all the rest. I'd been working for two years already; I knew the world I was made to live in. Yet now we were to be made to leave. We were to be made to walk. We didn't know for how long, or for what purpose. We were walking into the unknown.

It was July 26, 1944, and it was blazing hot. The light shuddered in visible, heaving waves; the air had a thickness to it, a dampness and density that settled on the skin and clung to it like wet wool.

I wore my blouse and sweater under my camp uniform.

We were given nothing for the journey—no food, no water. Just a massive column of people: men and women and a small number of young boys, too, walking closely together, too closely, I suspect, for the heat, looking about, looking down, all afraid, all exhausted before we even began, past the barbed-wire gates, and out onto the road. At first, I remember, I walked near Mima and Feter; perhaps my father was with us, too. I don't remember anyone speaking, or conversations of any kind.

The German soldiers walked on either side of the road. They carried guns and held dogs on leashes.

For three days, we walked in the ferocious summer heat. Perhaps we walked for four days; I don't know. One loses a sense of time when all the world contracts into the single project of taking yet another step, step after step, for kilometers on end. And the heat all around, the heat burning down from the heavens and rising up in waves from under the road. All the world transformed into an oven, a terrific furnace, and all of us enveloped in it, burning in its belly, with no one to offer us relief.

We dragged ourselves along in that heat, people eventually stripping off whatever clothes they had put on under their camp uniforms. It was too hot for extra clothes, too hot to be walking, each step along the hard surface a new affliction in one's legs. I know we walked close to one hundred kilometers, from Radom east, and slightly north, to Tomaszów Mazowiecki. At night, we lay in the wheat fields that lined the road, and the pointed tips of the harvested stalks pricked our skin as we sank into dreamless sleep.

On the second day of the march, or perhaps the third—I don't remember, only that I had been walking forever in the unrelenting anger of that heat—we came upon a small village with ramshackle houses set apart from each other by patches of yard and fences built from splintered wood. An odd quiet suffused the place—no wagons on the road making way for the thousands marching through, no one hammering on a roof, no children playing in a yard. Everyone was inside, protected, hidden in safety—except for a single woman I saw standing at the threshold of her house, staring blankly at us, as we dragged ourselves along in the heat.

Would no one offer us any help? No one with a spoonful of water? A drop of mercy for the Jews passing by?

A frightful thought came to me then—that I was absolutely alone, even amid the many hundreds of others walking alongside me, alone and without consequence in the world. That no one would want to protect me. That there was no safety left anywhere. I was alone and exposed on the open road.

Was this when it started? A thought barely conscious, a question unformed, simmering in my blood: Why go on?

A young boy was walking somewhat ahead of me. I didn't know him; I didn't remember having ever seen him in the area of the barracks, but I remember noticing that he was walking by himself, no mother with an arm around him hurrying him along, no father holding his hand. Seeing him made me wonder about another motherless boy I knew, a boy we called Shulem Szpitalnik, whom I and several others had taken care of in the barracks. I didn't see Shulem Szpitalnik at all on the march, and I wouldn't see him again until we arrived at Auschwitz.

But here was this other boy walking ahead of me. He knelt down by a puddle at the side of the road. Where did this puddle come from, I wonder? Certainly, there had been no rain. Perhaps someone had dumped a pail of dirty water from a house. Perhaps some water had splashed out of a bucket as someone was returning home from a nearby well. A puddle of dirty water—a miniature oasis in the summer heat. The boy knelt down and bent his head to the ground to take a sip. To lap up a drop of water. But this was not permitted; we were not allowed to linger in our march, even for a moment. Did he know this? I wondered. Did he know the cost of his desire for relief?

The boy knelt down and bent his body to the ground. A German guard came up to him, stood over him, impassively watching the boy lick the water. He took his gun from its holster, held it out before him, and then, without reprimand, without a word of any kind, the soldier shot the boy in the back of the head. The boy fell over onto his side. No one made a motion toward him. No one cried out or ran to pick up his body. We all just walked on, under the blazing sun.

At the back of the march, there was a horse-drawn wagon. It was a simple enough contraption, just a horse attached by harness to a wooden cart. A soldier sat on a plank above the cart and drove the wagon on. Several others walked alongside. This wagon, we were told, was provided for our comfort: If any of us felt tired, if we felt we could walk no longer, we were welcome to drop to the back of the march and ride on the wagon.

Mr. Goldberg was the first to get on. He was an older man, maybe sixty or more. My family knew him a little from Radom. He was wealthy before the war and generous, too: I know he had money with him in the KL; I heard that he was able to buy bread from the Poles and that he shared it with others in his barracks.

To share your bread when you yourself are starving—this is an extraordinary thing. It's important to consider this.

Mr. Goldberg got on the wagon. He was old, he was exhausted, and the heat was too much to bear. He needed a rest, a moment of respite. So he got on the wagon.

The soldier flicked the reins and turned the horse off the road. I watched the wagon head into the woods; I remember wondering why they would be taking a detour. Then I heard a single shot. Moments later, the wagon returned, empty.

I am trying to figure this out, if there is some logic here. Of course, nothing like this occurred to me then, but now, in my reflection, in my telling this little story, I have to wonder about the logic of that wagon. What idea underlies an order instructing soldiers to shoot on the spot anyone who bends down to lap up a tongueful of dirty water from the road, but then also orchestrates an elaborate farce about offered aid, about a free ride on a wagon, only to turn that wagon into a vehicle of death? The Germans were so meticulous about things. They kept records of everything. There's a book detailing the minutiae of the Radom deportations; they calculated exactly how many calories the Jewish workers in the factory should consume in a day. So in what meticulous plan did that wagon play a part? As much as they wanted to exterminate us, as much as by this time they had put into effect their Final

Solution, still they needed workers. Even at Auschwitz, we were known as the "ammunition workers," and every so often, some number of us would be selected and taken away to an armaments factory in Germany to work, as I eventually would be, in the winter of 1944–1945. They wanted to kill us all, I suppose, but still leave themselves just enough Jews to provide the slave labor they needed to keep the war machine alive.

So they weren't intent on murdering every one of us on that march; they were content to let die those who fell from exhaustion; they were content to kill outright those who could no longer bear the ordeal. But still, why the wagon? Why seduce us with the offer of comfort only to turn that offer into a means of murder? To this day, I cannot comprehend the reason for that wagon.

There were others, too, I know, others like Mr. Goldberg who went on the wagon. Nojich Tannenbaum, for example. Though with him it was different, for he didn't go himself on the wagon; he put his children there.

Tannenbaum was the informer, the one who boasted that he and his family would survive the war on an island of safety while all around them everything would be burning. He had such confidence, this Tannenbaum; he was so sure that the Germans would protect him for his services to them. Tannenbaum thought he was safe from what was happening to all the other Jews. But he was made to go on that march, too; he was sent to Auschwitz, just like the rest of us.

Tannenbaum walked along in the heat with his family. His twin girls were maybe two or three years old at the time, too young to walk on their own. So Tannenbaum carried one of them on his shoulders, and the maid carried the other one. And I suppose it got too hard for him, carrying his child all that distance. So he told the maid—her last name was Helfand, I remember; she was a Jew, too, a girl from our town—he told her to put the child she carried down on the wagon and he would put the other one down, too. And that's what they did: They put the two little girls on the wagon.

I didn't get to see what happened after that—if the little girls cried as their father left them. Perhaps they thought they were being treated to something special, to ride along on a wagon while everyone else had to walk. What did he say to them as he put them down? What could he possibly have said? I don't know. I didn't see. Nor did I see what happened with his wife, if she went crazy in anger or fright, if he had to calm her or try somehow to justify what he had done. Had she concurred with this plan? Had she agreed to his putting their children on that wagon?

There were too many horrors happening to think of these things, to consider the weight, the meaning of these things. Of a boy shot for thirst, of a father giving up his babies to die. A girl I knew, Luba Lastman, I saw run off into the high wheat fields, hoping to escape, I assume. She was the daughter of the family who owned the apartment building we lived in on Wolnosc Street. She was maybe twenty years old, young and strong; she must have thought she could outrun the soldiers. But the Germans followed her in with their dogs, sniffing, barking, straining at their leashes. I heard the shot in the near distance.

And we just kept walking, everyone in his own world, everyone with his own troubles, everyone under the flaming sun.

For me, it was my thighs. Walking in that impossible, scorching heat. I had taken off my blouse and sweater early on. I wasn't going to escape—nobody could escape—so what need did I have for civilian clothes? But even just with the disheveled dress I wore, the heat was unbearable. As I was walking, with the sweat and the dirt, my thighs rubbed one against the other. With every step, they rubbed back and forth, catching against the sweat. All those steps, all those kilometers. Soon the rubbing raised sores between my legs, and the sores soon opened and bled. And there was nothing to do, nothing to ease the pain. I had just to keep walking, in that heat, with no water, my feet aching, my legs bleeding. My body pulled to the earth by the weight of its own fatigue.

So when was this? Still the second day, perhaps. Something broke in me, broke off in my brain and vanished. A will, perhaps, a determination to move forward, to get to the next place, the next stage of whatever path I was on. At some point, this no longer existed for me. And in its place, the question: Why go on? For what? To where? I couldn't go on anymore; I couldn't walk anymore in so much pain. The heat and the thirst and the searing fire between my legs—it was too much. I was done. I gave up. I was content to climb onto the wagon.

Where was my family? Mima and Feter and my father? I don't think I saw them; in any event, I wasn't aware of them. I don't think they knew what I was doing; I have to believe they would have tried to stop me.

It was simple, really. I turned around and started to walk back, against the flow of the hundreds of people walking behind me. No one minded me, no one asked why I was walking

in the wrong direction. They realized, they didn't realize—
who knows? Everyone was consumed in his own misery, as I
was consumed in mine.

I reached the wagon. It was a relief to me, that wagon. A
place to rest, a place to find an end to the torture down my
legs. Not a place of death, no, just the opposite. The wagon
was respite, an end to the ordeal of walking. It was where the
pain would stop, where the bright lightning down my legs
would cease. I craved that wagon more than I had craved anything in my life. It was my sole focus, the concentrated point
of all my energy, to climb onto that wagon and find my rest.

I lay my hands on the wooden boards, taking a step or two in
time with the wagon's movement so I could hoist myself up. No
thinking now, no reflection. Walking in time with the movement of the wheels, with the clopping of the horses' hooves,
myself synchronized with the wagon and about to get on.

And then, under my arms, other arms holding me. Hands in
my armpits holding me firmly and pulling me back, dragging
me away from the wagon.

The wagon moved forward; I dimly watched it go.

Two people kept me from death; I had no idea who they
were.

Did I faint at that point? Collapse into the support of whoever was holding me upright? I remember two young men on
either side of me; I remember them holding me, drawing me
forward, back into that mass of people traipsing along on an
endless road.

What followed is indistinct to me, a memory muffled in an
emptiness that didn't go away. I had been brought back from
the edge, but I have no sense, even now, that I was grateful for

the effort. I had given up, and even in my return, I remained as I was, drained of all effort, spent, exhausted, done.

I remember Mima scolding me, but it was like calling out into a void, a voice without resonance, to no avail. Before us, we simply had more of the same—more heat, more thirst, more of the march. There was nothing to be done but follow along with everyone else.

After one hundred kilometers, we reached the town of Tomaszów. The Germans separated the men from the women—the men were taken down the road to a building that looked like a run-down factory; the women were pushed into an abandoned warehouse.

We had heard rumors about the gas. Nothing was certain, but we had heard that there were places like Treblinka, where the Germans were sending Jews to be gassed to death. So when the women saw their men herded into this factory, they thought this was it, this was the place where their husbands and brothers, their fathers and their sons, were going to die. The men would be shoved into this building, and the gas would be turned on, and they would be forced to suck in the poisoned air. It was, in the end, just an abandoned building, but the women didn't know that then.

So they began to scream.

Women exhausted, women on the verge of collapse, were suddenly transformed, erupting with an energy all but absent moments before. Shrieking, crying, "Where are you taking them? What is happening to my husband?" Calling out, wild-eyed, as we were driven into this warehouse, some hundreds of women pushed into this cavernous building. After the torment of the march came the nightmare of women watching their men and boys being sent to what the women thought was their death.

And all around us, the Germans, with their guns and their dogs.

We were pushed inside; then the Germans left and locked the doors behind them.

The warehouse was windowless, dark, and it smelled stale. We sat down wherever we could—on the floor, on benches— it didn't matter. We had marched for days; we were locked in an airless and barren place with guards standing outside the doors; we didn't know what was going to happen to us or what was happening even now to our men. But we were being allowed to rest. That, at least, was a gift.

Then came the lice. All of a sudden, out of nowhere, an invasion like the plagues in Egypt. All at once, everyone was up and shrieking, frantically tearing at their skin. The lice were all over us, swarming about our heads and over our bodies. I remember jumping wildly, trying in vain to push them off, to swipe them down and off of me. Nothing worked. The place was infested, and soon so were we.

We went to sleep that night, our bodies alive with insects. It would take the *Entlaussung*—the "delousing"—of Auschwitz to rid ourselves of the vermin.

※

When I was growing up in Radom—before the ghetto, before the war—I used to walk to school every day with another girl, Mila Rosenbaum. I would stop by her apartment on my way and wait for her to collect her things so we could go off together.

She was the youngest in a large family with many brothers and sisters. The next child up was a boy named Heniek; there were older siblings, too, but I didn't know them as well, because they were so much older than I. One, I remembered, Leon, worked at the factory in Radom.

Mila and Heniek both survived the war; Mila settled in Israel, Heniek in Toronto. Jack and I kept in touch with them both. Once, many years after the war, Jack and I were visiting Heniek in Toronto—for a bar mitzvah, I think, or perhaps for someone's wedding. We sat in his living room, talking about this and that, nothing special, when one of Heniek's brothers, Leon Rosenbaum, came over to me and asked if I remembered him. Yes, I said, of course I did. He was one of Mila's older brothers; I remembered him from their apartment when I used to wait for Mila on the way to school, and from the factory, too, during the war; I remember he worked at the kuznia. But this was not what he was talking about. "Don't you remember," Leon asked me, "that time on the march to Tomaszów? That time when I pulled you away from the wagon?"

Unbelievable. In all those years, I never knew who it was who had put his hands under my arms to keep me from that wagon. During all those years of friendship with Heniek, I had no idea it was his brother who had kept me that day from death.

Leon then told me who the other boy was, but I didn't write down his name and I don't remember it now. I wish I could name him.

I never thought much of my own stories. I don't think it ever even came up with Heniek, that story about the wagon. We were all survivors and everyone had stories; everyone had private horrors and near escapes from death. We talked about the war all the time—even today, we talk about it endlessly among ourselves. But it's never a presentation, a detailed exposition, like, "Here, I'm going to tell you a story about what happened to me."

So I never mentioned to Heniek what had happened on the march, and I never wrote down the name of the other boy who had pulled me from that wagon. But at least I got to know about Leon; at least I got to thank Leon, directly, for what he had done.

10

Somehow—oddly, perhaps—it's the boots that matter most. Maybe it's because of those cursed clogs I was given in their place, which tore at my feet and made them bleed. Or maybe it's because the boots were from home, a remnant of Radom taken from me. Perhaps. All I know is that when I got to Auschwitz and I was made to undress, I had to give up my boots—soft, brown leather, lace-up boots that came up high on my calves. I had to take them off and throw them onto an enormous heap of footwear—shoes and boots, all worn and rough, piling up in an ever-growing mound, the plunder of war. Seeing that vast and growing pile, I knew that whatever was going to befall me in this place, I was never going to see my boots again; I was never going to get my boots back. That was terrible to me, an indecency, to be bereft of my own boots.

〜

The rolling doors of the metal boxcar slide open, and I have a brief moment of relief, almost of hope. I have heard rumors about Auschwitz, vague suspicions about it being a death camp, about people being forced to breathe poisoned gas, and the few days I have spent on the train from Tomaszów to Auschwitz have made these rumors seem real. Has it been two days? Three? No food or water, the car crowded so densely there was no place to crouch, the air rank with the smell of urine and feces steaming in the sweltering heat. It felt like death inside that train; it felt as if we were riding that train toward death. I prayed to a God I barely believed in that at my death, I would not feel pain.

When the doors slide open, everyone comes pouring out. Hundreds of us, the withered along with the dead, spewed out at once from fetid cars. Dogs are barking, soldiers shouting orders I can't understand, but there, above the gates, I read the words wrought in metal that confirm my uncle's teaching: *Arbeit macht frei.* I don't know German well, but the phrase is close enough to Yiddish for me to understand: Work makes you free. This is what Feter routinely says, or close enough, anyway. If you work, you will survive. This is why I went to the factory in the first place; this is why I grudgingly consented to return there after going back to the ghetto and getting the feather blanket. For years already, everyone has been desperate to find work, and now here we are, the surviving ammunition workers from Radom, come into the fresh air after unendurable days in a closed car, come to a new camp to work for the war.

But my minute of hope ends nearly before it has begun. Men in uniform are coming at us with hard rubber batons, jabbing people in the gut, whacking at our backs, barking at us orders to separate—men here, women over there. Everyone suddenly is frantic, not knowing what is unfolding in our midst. Mima and I watch Feter, Moishele, and my father being pushed along into the mass of men hustled away from us.

Mima calls out, "Szrul! Take care of our son!"

Now it is just the women. The selection begins—to the right, to the left. Families further torn apart. I see a friend of mine, Hilda Schwartz, furiously clutching at her mother. The guards are pulling her mother away, rough-handling her, beating both of them with their sticks. Hilda doesn't want to let go; she's in a rage, crying, clawing at her mother's dress, holding on like someone over the edge of a cliff, desperate to keep her grip on solid earth, desperate not to fall into the emptiness beneath. And the guards, the soldiers—whoever they are, the Germans—they're pounding at them, mother and daughter both, as Hilda vainly tries to hold on.

(The fierceness of that love! How unrelenting, how heroic, and no less for its futility. A daughter's true devotion; I admire that so.)

Hilda's mother is dragged away.

The place is all chaos. Wailing children are shoved next to bewildered women not their mothers to try, futilely, to calm them, to quiet them down. The Germans want to kill us, it seems, but they don't want to deal with our screams. The little boy, Shulem Szpitalnik, goes like this, paired off with a woman he's never seen before.

Shulem Szpitalnik. That wasn't his real name; it's the name we gave because he never told us his own.

It was in Radom during the previous spring, and I was returning with the women to the barracks from my shift at the factory. I noticed a sad-faced boy walking alone and aimlessly. He was maybe five or six years old and looked utterly bewildered to be wandering all by himself. I took his hand and gently guided him into the row of women walking back. He came along easily, quietly, sandwiched between me and Mima, grateful, it seemed, to be led.

When we got back to the barracks, all the women crowded around.

"What's your name, little boy?" "Where's your mother?"

We wanted to know where he came from and what he was doing out on the streets all alone. But he wouldn't answer us; he didn't say a word.

Someone thought maybe he was deaf; maybe he wasn't answering us because he couldn't hear our questions. So she threw a shoe down hard against the floor to make a big noise and see if he would react. He did—he startled at the sound, but still he didn't say anything. He looked more resolute than scared, content to be indoors with a group of women hovering about him, but determined not to speak. Perhaps, we thought, he was obeying a lesson his mother taught him; perhaps his mother had told him never to talk to people he didn't know.

In all the months he was with us, we never found out anything about this boy—his name, his age, where he came from, or how he wound up walking alone on the streets. He never said a word to any of us. But we took him in and cared for him, as best we could, during the time we had left in Radom. We fed him from our bits of bread and broth, and we gave him a name that he eventually responded to. He hid himself at night in the barracks that served as a kind of clinic. In Yiddish, the word for "hospital" is *spitual*, so we called him Shulem Szpitalnik, the peaceable boy who hid in a hospital. The name was more than a way to call out to him; it was a way to hold him in our hearts.

I so admired this boy. He never complained and he never cried. And he was smart, too: He seemed always to know without being told when it was safe for him to be seen and when he needed to disappear. During the appels, for example, he knew that he mustn't be spotted when we were being counted in the evenings after work. When the appel was disbanded, he'd suddenly reappear in the barracks and come to us for a sip of soup. We were hungry all the time, with not enough food for ourselves, but we gave to him, anyway, because he was young and he was helpless, and offering him bits of our food, offering him what small protection we could, must have in some small way made us feel human.

He walked with us on the march to Tomaszów—one hundred kilometers, and he didn't give up. And he rode with us on the train to Auschwitz. All alone and with no one he would speak to.

What a remarkable child he was. I so wanted him to survive.

And now the selection. We're being sorted out. To the left, to the right. To the camp, to the gas. Shulem Szpitalnik is shoved over to a woman he doesn't know, and she now takes him hesitantly by the hand. And they go together, the two of them, hand in hand, to their death.

☙❧

Chaos. Frenzy. Fear.

We are told to undress. Undress? In the open? With every-one around? For what? Why should we have to undress? We have been counted before; we have been lined up before, but never without clothes, never naked.

We have things. Not much, but little things, little things we have brought with us, for memory's sake, or for the sake of safety. We want to be able to hide these things.

Szlamek Horowitz's mother approaches me. She tells me that she is wearing under her dress a small belt made of cloth into which she has sewn little pockets. In the pockets, she has hidden away several diamonds. Perhaps she will be able to buy some bread with these stones; perhaps she will be able to buy her life. She asks me, Will I hide this belt for her? Will I hide her little diamonds? If I do, if I agree, she says, we will be part-ners: She will split the diamonds with me, and both of us will be able to buy some bread. Perhaps both of us will be able to buy our lives. I want to say yes; really, I do. But I can't. I'm afraid. I know I can't keep anything from the Germans; they will find out, surely, and instead of saving my life, the dia-monds will be the end of it. I will be beaten; I will be killed. I cannot, I am sorry, I am too afraid.

And where can we hide anything, anyway? We are being told to undress, to strip naked.

I, too, have things to hide—my picture, my rings. But where will I hide them if I have to give up my underwear?

I hear a man calling out a woman's name.

"Jadzia, Jadzia, come here!"

The man is from Radom, already interned in Auschwitz, and he has come to meet this transport of Radomers to see if he can find anyone from his family—his mother or a sister, perhaps, maybe his wife. He doesn't find anyone from his family, but he knows this woman, Jadzia, and he tells her he has something to give her. He has a pocket watch; he was hoping to give it to someone in his family, but now he doesn't think he'll ever find any of them. So he wants to give the watch to Jadzia; perhaps it will help her. It's a gold watch in a case that opens up from either side. I'm sure it's worth a lot of money. Jadzia takes the watch and returns to our group. Surrounded by women, she lifts the bottom of her dress and reaches underneath. She pushes the watch up into her vagina. High up. All the way in.

"They will not search me there," she says. "The watch will be safe in there."

Jadzia was right, as it turned out. When we were inspected later on, they checked between our fingers, between our toes, in our mouths. But not in our vaginas. We were spared this, I assume, not because of the degradation of an inspection there—the degradations were so many that day in Auschwitz—but because of the time it would take to inspect so many women in that particular way. There were many hundreds of women in the Tomaszów transport, and for the German commanders and their inmate officers, there was much to be done with us, and there was no time for lengthy inspections.

Jadzia was able to keep her pocket watch, but later, when we were in the barracks, she was unable to get it out. Lying on the bunk—the *prycza*, it was called, rough wooden slats laid side to side, eight women crammed together on each prycza at night—she reached in, trying to get a firm hold. Then she pulled, gently at first, I suspect, but maybe then not so gently. It wouldn't come out; it was stuck. She dug into her insides, she yanked at the fob, but nothing worked. Maybe she had swollen up; maybe the watch had gotten lodged on a bit of pelvic bone. Whatever it was, it wouldn't come out. And it was terrible, she suffered so. Days and days, fishing around inside herself. She asked her best friend to try, and she did; others, too—other women from the barracks went between her legs, mucking around inside her for that watch. Nothing helped; no one could get it out. She got an infection, night after night screaming in pain. I don't know how she got through the days. She cried out to us, just to kill her. She didn't want to go to the *revier*, the so-called infirmary; she knew that no one came out from there. She preferred to die in the barracks, with her friends about her.

"Just kill me," she said. "I don't care anymore. I cannot take this pain."

Perhaps this is odd: I don't remember how Jadzia finally got the pocket watch out of herself—whether she managed to remove it herself or whether someone else did. What I remember is her torture, the price she paid for trying to give herself a little protection.

Jadzia survived the war; I don't know what happened to the watch.

Mima also has a place for hiding things—her ankle boots, which for some reason she is allowed to keep. In the heel of one, she has sealed up her little gold ring. But she has a picture, too, of her children—of Chava, who has already been killed, and of Moishele, whom she has just seen taken away

150

Mima and Feter's children, Chava and Moishele,
in the photograph that Mima hid in her ankle boot

with Feter. More than anything, Mima wants to keep this
picture, the faces of her children in black and white. So she
takes off one of her shoes and gently tugs at the inner
lining, carefully lifting the thin strip of leather from the
undersole.

I see what she is doing. I have a picture, too; I, too, want to keep this picture.

"Mima, will you take my picture? Will you keep it for me?"

"Of course, Maniusia, of course."

So she takes my treasured picture, sliding it with hers under the bottom lining of her shoe. And both pictures—one of two young children, the other of two young newlyweds—stay there, hidden in Mima's shoe, slightly creased, all through the rest of the war.

I have Mima's picture of Chava and Moishele, framed, hanging on my wall; until now, I have kept my own picture to myself.

But then the rings. What of my wedding rings? I want these, too; I want these especially. I have kept these rings hoping Heniek and I might one day be able to wear them again, hoping we might one day again be husband and wife. I know, I suppose, that Heniek is dead, that I will never see him again. But still I hope. How can I give up my hope if I cannot give up my longing? I want the rings so I can hold on to hope, so I can hold on to him, my husband, my Heniek.

What am I to do? I cannot put the rings in the heel of Mima's shoe—that space was sealed when the shoes were made. So where can I hide them?

There is a woman among us, also named Jadzia, but a different woman from the first. Her name is Jadzia Fetman, and she's from Warsaw, not Radom. She and her sister Carolla came to the Radom factory several months ago, and I've known her already for some time. She's strong and fearless, even gruff in her manner, but she's kind, too; I know that. I tell her about the rings. I tell her that I want to keep them, but I have no place to hide them. I realize I have to get rid of them; I tell Jadzia that I'm going to throw them down, in the dirt. I won't have them, but at least the Germans won't have them, either.

And then, again, a kindness from nowhere, an unrequited goodness, an act of purity in a sullied place.

"Mania. I will take the rings. I will hide them for you."

And she does. Jadzia takes my rings, and she reaches under her grimy striped dress, and she puts my wedding rings up into her vagina. And she keeps them there throughout that terrible day, my thin gold wedding rings, my treasures, hidden in the warmth of her insides.

I don't remember when Jadzia gave the rings back to me. Nor do I remember how I managed to keep them with me during my months in Auschwitz. My memories of Auschwitz—of the entire war, really—come only in pieces. Stray anecdotes, interrupted narratives, bits of conversation. I remember that I had these rings and didn't know how I could keep them, and I remember the wondrous kindness of Jadzia to do something dangerous and indecent to help me. I know at some point I got the rings back. I have them still.

We stand naked, hundreds of Radom women in the middle of an enormous compound. The place is teeming with naked women. What is happening to us, to be naked in so public a place? To be so completely exposed. The Germans are all about, with their dogs and their rubber batons, swiping at us at random. The camp guards—Jews even—are no better than their captors.

When I was at Beis Yaakov, the Jewish grammar school for girls—it seems a lifetime ago; it seems some other world (for it is, it is)—I was taught how to be modest. My teacher was a beautiful and pious woman, and when she prayed in the corner of the room, her face turned to the wall, her body gently pitching forward and back in time with the rhythms of her soft chanting, she seemed so focused, so fervent in her quiet devotion, I was sure that she was speaking directly to God. My family, too, of course, but this woman most especially taught me modesty—that I should be covered, dresses below my knees, sleeves below my elbows, and this seemed right to me—though, of course, I never would have questioned it, anyway. It seemed right to me for a girl to be covered in this way. It was a sign of humility and decency to be modest in one's dress.

In Auschwitz, I am utterly exposed. I don't know where to put my hands—there is too much of me for my meager hands to cover. My breasts, my bottom; the front of me, the back. Where to cast my eyes? I don't want to look at anybody; I don't want anybody to look at me. I want to evaporate; I want to dissolve into the air.

We are taken to be shaved. We stand in line before a row of women, Jewish inmates they are, standing across from us with straight razors in their hands. Each in turn, we stand before them, and each one of us gets shaved. Everywhere. Our heads, under our arms, between our legs.

"Arms up! Spread your legs!"

Razors scraping against skin. Razors scratching, nicking the flesh. Little pellets of blood rise up on my stinging skin. I ask, timidly, tentatively, "Please, will you save some hair on my head?" I have always had such fine hair—baby hair, I call it. Silly, I suppose, to be concerned about so small a thing. Sillier still to think that my simple request might ever be granted. The woman grabs my hair in her fist, pulls hard, yanking up the skin of my scalp, and swipes her razor across my head. She cuts off my hair; she slices off a small piece of my scalp.

಄

In the Auschwitz museum—I visited there in 1987—there are rooms filled with the things the Germans confiscated from the Jews: thousands of suitcases, a storeroom of eyeglasses, shoes of every size, a mountain of human hair. All that hair, shaved from all those heads. And attached at the ends of those fragile strands, for a time, at any rate, little bits of scalp, shards of Jewish skin.

Eventually my hair grew back, except for in that one place where my skin was shorn. The skin grew back, but never the hair.

಄

Next, the Entlaussung, the delousing.

Again, we stand before Jewish inmates—hard, harsh women, willing to do such atrocious things.

Again, "Arms up! Legs open!"

They dunk dirty rags into buckets of some liquid—a disin-fectant, a delousing agent. The woman before me lifts her rag dripping with the stuff. I am no one to her—a naked body without a history, without a name. I am no different from the hundreds—surely the thousands—who have stood before her. Today, yesterday, last week, last year. This woman works blindly at her station as I worked at mine at the factory. I am a nothingness before her. She slaps the rags up and down my naked body. Liquid fire, acid eating away at my bleeding skin. My head, my underarms. Between my legs—so private, those parts, so delicate, throbbing now, scorching. I am aflame. My body on fire.

This is Auschwitz, this indignity, this torture. Everyone knows this now; everyone knows now about the nightmare of Auschwitz, about the walking skeletons, about the crema-toria, about the Final Solution. Nowadays you see a picture of naked, shaven women standing dazed in a barren yard somewhere in Auschwitz, and the image is horrifying, of course, but by now it is familiar, too. Everyone has seen these pictures; our children have been raised on them. But then, we didn't know about any of this. These insults to our bodies, to ourselves—to our sense of our selves—they shocked us just as much as they were degrading and filled with pain. That first day in Auschwitz was filled with things that seemed insane: Someone put a pocket watch in her vagina! Who does this? In what kind of world is someone made to do this? We had lived through the war already for five years. We had been through much; all of us had been through much.

But until now, we had lived in a world that we recognized—a frightening world, a cruel world, to be sure, but it was a world we could understand, too. The reality of Auschwitz was unrecognizable. These affronts stunned us, tore us brutally from anything we were able to decipher for ourselves, and dropped us into the panicked insanity of this horrible, horrifying place.

And then the showers. How can I describe this? Hundreds of us, petrified and disoriented, driven into a cement-walled chamber.

There are round spigots hanging from the ceiling. This is a gas chamber; I am sure of it. We have been herded into this room to be gassed. I am going to be gassed.

My heart is pounding, my breath is fast and shallow. My mouth is so parched my tongue sticks to my teeth. I wait moment by moment for the end, for the gas, to breathe poison. I look up at the spigots, watching for the gas. Will it burn my insides, that first breath? Will it take long for me to die? This waiting is the worst, the anticipation of the physical torture to come.

Women are screaming, wailing. Hundreds of women huddled together on the verge of a massive murder. I cling to Mima, her arms wrapped around me. We will be together when we die. But I want Mama. More than ever, I want to be with my mother. It is horrible—I can't say it another way—it is horrible to be in this room waiting for the gas.

The spigots open, and out of them—water. Scalding hot, then freezing cold, then hot and cold again. But water, not gas. Water.

We emerge from that chamber transformed. Truly, we can barely recognize each other; without hair, we all look like men. We gaze into each other's eyes to see if we can see ourselves in someone else's pupils. We want to know what we look like—shorn and swollen, devastated, but grateful, too, for we haven't been killed.

Each of us is given a dress. You get whatever is handed to you. Tall women get short dresses, short women get long ones. No bra, no panties. Just a dress. For shoes I got a pair of wooden clogs that had never been sanded or smoothed out on the insides. It was an unequaled agony, walking barefoot in these clogs. I have nightmares about them even now.

I lost my period at Auschwitz, and I said it was a blessing. What would I have done with a period? How would I have managed that?

11

I REMAINED IN AUSCHWITZ FOR ALMOST SIX MONTHS, FROM July 1944 until just before the end of the year. Auschwitz was a daily dread: The threat of death, of being "selected," was with us every day. We saw the smoke of the crematoria; we knew what was possible. Twice a day, we stood for the appels; every so often, we were made to stand naked, and an SS officer would come to look us over and select women from the line. I always stood with my head bent down, trying to cover myself with my eyes.

Auschwitz is now called an extermination camp, a death factory. Ten thousand people were killed in a single day in Auschwitz—more than one million people in all. It looked like death there—skeletal bodies, sunken eyes, black smoke from the chimneys. And the stench, the stench of what was burning. Nothing grew at Auschwitz. The place was more barren than a desert, as if nature itself knew that Auschwitz was the kingdom of death. Not a tree or a shrub, not a blade of grass. Not a fly. Nothing. Auschwitz was the end of the world, death's domain.

I had no sense then of the overall operation of the place, no awareness of its intricate structures, its hierarchies of power and systems of barbarity and barter. I knew only my own experience; I had only my own partial, incomplete view. People needed to survive; no one had the means to survive. Violence was the norm. My months at Auschwitz were focused on only what mattered most—food, shoes, staying unnoticed. I had my aunt, and I had a good deal of luck. I cannot describe what Auschwitz was "like," for it was like nothing else that ever was; I can offer only pieces, those that live in me still.

ℵℶ

I was hungry all the time. Every morning, we got tepid brown liquid and a slice of hard bread. After the evening appel, we were given thin broth. Every day, the same; every day, not enough to calm the pain gnawing at my gut. My hunger was like an animal I carried inside, an animal that periodically unfurled its claws and scraped at the edges of my belly. It might lie quiet for a time, perhaps when I was talking with Mima or focused on some small labor. But not often, and never for long. That scraping, that digging, that pain inside my gut—it never went away. It was there when I went to sleep at night, and it greeted me as soon as I awoke in the morning. In Auschwitz, bread was precious beyond measure, precious nearly beyond love.

But maybe not quite. Or not for everyone.

Not, at least, for Mima.

Mima, 1932

Everyone needed a partner in Auschwitz, someone to watch out for you, someone to hold your bowl and spoon when you went to the latrine. Mima was my partner. I don't know during those days and months at Auschwitz if I provided any solace for my aunt, if my life and her daily determination to protect it gave her any strength, any inner resolve to hold on.

I hope they did; I really do hope her care for me was good for her, because I know with perfect clarity how good it was for me. I know what would have happened to me in Auschwitz without her.

After we got our slice of bread in the mornings, my habit was to take just two bites and then leave the rest for the duration of the day and into the next morning. I wanted to take the last nibble of bread just before we got our next day's portion. I was frightened to be without food, even if it was only a single bite of bread. The others used to scold me: "You'll never feel full this way. You must eat your full portion so you won't starve." But I never knew what the next day would bring—would there be food tomorrow? Would we get another piece of bread? So I preferred to have my bread this way—two small bites in the morning, a bite or two during the day, a piece left over for when I woke up.

I needed to keep the bread overnight. I couldn't simply hold it, because it might fall out of my hand while I slept and then surely someone would pick it up and eat it herself. My dress, of course, had no pockets. So Mima let me use her shoe. Mima and I shared the same bunk, and at night, we used her shoes as pillows. We had to sleep on them because they, too, would have been stolen—everything in Auschwitz you didn't hold on to was immediately stolen. So at night, Mima and I slept on her shoes, each of us with one hand on the shoe under our own cheek, and the other hand holding the shoe under the cheek of the other; this way, we would be sure to know if someone tried to take either shoe while we slept. Nestled together in this way at night, we protected our possessions: One shoe under Mima's head held her ring in its heel; the other, under mine, held two pictures under its lining and a crust of bread at its toe.

Mima was my partner, too, for the appels. Though we were known as the ammunition workers, we weren't given much to do at the camp. At some point, we realized that we were being kept in reserve for transport to factories inside Germany that needed slave labor. In the meantime, our days were taken up mostly by the appels, which lasted several hours each, once in the morning and once again in the evening. We were made to line up in rows outside our barracks, and whatever the weather, we stood and waited to be counted.

A woman from our barracks, Mrs. Lax, collapsed once during an appel. It was summer and ferociously hot. She was between forty and fifty years old, and she couldn't remain standing so long in the heat. The guard saw her collapse, and she was punished for her weakness.

Mrs. Lax was told to kneel on the stony ground while holding a brick in each hand with her arms outstretched. When she dropped her arms to her sides or fell from her bleeding knees to rest—as happened once or twice—the guard beat her with a stick and restarted her timing from the begining. How long did Mrs. Lax have to stay that way? After two minutes, your arms are on fire; after two hours?

The rest of us from the barracks had to stand in our rows and watch, striving to keep our strength so that we, too, wouldn't fall.

Mima knew I had a tendency to faint. I was small to begin with, and I had lost a lot of weight. Every so often, sometimes during an appel, but sometimes just during the day, the world would all of a sudden get hazy before me and I would black out. Once, after I had fainted, a woman I knew slightly from the Radom factory—she was a twin, and she had been experimented on by Mengele—saw me on the ground and came over to me and offered me a little piece of raw potato she had. It was to help me wake up, she said. This matters, I think—that such kindness was possible, even in Auschwitz. If a guard saw me fainting during an appel, however, I would certainly be punished, and if a selection were to occur and someone saw the paleness of my face, I might get taken away to be gassed.

Mima always had with her a little bit of red brick. How did she manage that? I wonder. Was it the same piece through all those months, or did she scavenge bits and pieces from the ground? I don't know.

There is so much I don't know.

If Mima saw that I looked too white, if she thought I was about to faint, she would take her bit of brick and rub it hard against my cheeks. She wanted to redden me. She wanted to disguise my pallor. The rubbing brought some color back to my cheeks and turned them the color of the brick, too—it would rub off on my ashen skin. Rough rouge in a death camp.

It was during the appels, too, that women were chosen for transport. Everyone wanted to go. We didn't know where the chosen women would be taken—we were told to factories to make guns—but any place was better than this; to be taken for a transport was a ticket out of hell.

Here, too, Mima was always thinking about me. Twice she was chosen for a transport; twice she had the chance to leave.

But each time, she positioned herself at the back of the gathering group, and when she saw that I was not part of the transport, she slipped away and stayed behind. To be with me. To lend me her shoe for a pillow. To redden my cheeks with a bit of brick. To take care of me.

Mima saw to my shoes as well. She knew how I suffered from those wooden clogs. My feet were a mess of splinters and sores from the endless rubbing of the rough wood against my bare skin. One day, a truck passed through our section of the camp. Its open back was piled high with shoes, the shoes of girls and women who had been killed, girls and women who had been gassed. Shoes of the dead.

In an instant, Mima ran to the truck, jumped up alongside it, and snatched a pair of shoes from the back. She could have been beaten for that—killed, even; many, many people were killed for less. But no one saw, or no one cared.

She brought the shoes back for me.

They were children's shoes, maybe three sizes too small. But I didn't mind. They were real leather shoes, and no matter how small, they were infinitely better than the clogs. I untied the laces and pushed my feet in. I had to curl my toes under to get my feet to fit. And I had to walk that way, too—with my toes curled under. And this gave me cramps, to walk with my toes curled. To this day, my feet aren't right—my toes grew deformed from some young girl's shoes. But they were shoes. Real leather shoes that Mima had risked her life to steal for me.

Why was Mima not as afraid of our captors as I was? I was so frightened all the time.

The commander of our barracks section was a Jewish woman from Czechoslovakia; she wasn't much older than I—

in her early twenties, I would guess—but she was hardened and cruel, and it pleased her to demean us. *Radomske kurwa*—Radomer whore—she called each of us. That's the greeting she used the very first time she came into our barracks, and she called us whores routinely afterward. We were already so humiliated, why did she have to add this slur to our disgrace? When winter came and the cold tore at us, digging its fingers deep into our chests, when we were maybe just a little slow to get outside to stand for our endless appels, she would come into our barracks and beat us with her stick, curse us as whores, and make us move faster.

Such gratuitous cruelty. And from a Jew. She had dull gray-blue eyes, I remember, and a flattened, open face that hid nothing, though there seemed really nothing to her, no dreams, no desires, other than her routine brutality. She was cruel in an almost casual way, as if her malice were a habit and not something that arose only in outbursts, in sudden response to some infraction, real or perceived. Her viciousness was her essence.

Was this woman so vicious all her life? Was Auschwitz only an outlet to enact a barbarity that already existed? Or did Auschwitz create this cruelty in her?

Does it matter?

The woman scared me to my core.

One might think that women guards would be kinder than men, gentler in their treatment of other human beings. But in my experience, this wasn't true. The women guards, Jews as well as the SS, were no less sadistic.

Once, just after a selection had ended and those of us not taken away were starting to disperse from our ranks to head back to our barracks, a group of women guards came after us, yelling at us to run, to get out of their way, to get back to our barracks. Everyone scrambled in different directions, following their command as best we could. I, too, started at once to run, but I couldn't move fast enough. My little leather shoes were too small for me; they made it hard to run. I was trying, though; I was. I was running for dear life, trying to get out of the guards' way. They were chasing us with some kind of stick in their hands—walking sticks, I suppose, because the sticks had pointed nails at their tip. I stumbled and fell. One of the guards caught up with me. She stood over me there on the ground; breathing hard, she lifted her stick in the air and began to smack me with it. She beat me on my head, my neck, my back.

The world is awry; this is what I mean when I say that Auschwitz was unrecognizable, even to us, even as we lived it. How was I to make sense of this woman beating me—I was doing what she said; I was running out of her way, just as the guards had commanded. But then, no one thought to make sense of these things—Jews treating other Jews with ferocity, SS guards delivering punishments without cause. No one tried to explain anything. All our attention, all our energy, was directed toward the most elemental issues—how to hold on to one's bread, how to stay standing for one minute more, how never to get noticed by anyone looking your way.

One time, quite early on, we were moved to a different area of the camp. I don't know why they moved us—we weren't told and we had nothing more to do in the new area than we had before. In our new barracks, we saw in the middle of the room a barrel filled with boiled potatoes. The women were all excited—food! An unexpected godsend. The potatoes were still warm, as if they had just been given to whoever lived in this barracks before us, women who must have just been taken away. The potatoes were the food of the dead, but we didn't care. To us they were a godsend still. Everyone ran to the barrel, reaching in to grab a potato. But then, after just a bite, everyone spit it out, coughing, gnashing her teeth. There was something wrong with the potatoes; they were rotten, or poisoned in some way.

A second barrel was in the barracks—this one was to be our latrine. I needed to use it, but it was too tall for me. I couldn't reach my bottom to its top. So I decided to sneak out. It was nighttime, and I thought perhaps I might find a corner of the yard to relieve myself unnoticed. Another girl thought the same, and we crept out together. She ran first, I followed just behind her. She found a place in the darkness; I, unfortunately, was discovered by a guard. The woman grabbed me by the top of my dress and paused for a moment, a second only, to look at me. Such hatred I don't think I had ever seen. I was disgusting to her, revolting, worth nothing at all. She raised her hand and struck me hard on the side of my head with her open palm. I fell to the ground, my ear ringing sharply and searing inside. I think she tore my eardrum, because for months afterward, I couldn't hear in that ear.

I had only gone out to urinate. What, dear God, was so hateful about that?

Life is supposed to make sense. Even cruelty, even when unjustified, should still make some sense; it should still be possible to explain according to some rationale. An explanation is not the same as an excuse; I'm not talking about morality here. I'm talking about a simple human expectation that there are reasons for human action. But in Auschwitz, nothing made sense.

In Auschwitz, I lost whatever was left of my faith.

When I was growing up, my faith was simple, but it was pure. As a child, I had watched my teacher at Beis Yaakov praying in the corner every day, and I trusted in her devotion; I believed that there was a God listening to her private prayers. From my grandparents, from my schooling, from my life in Radom, I was brought up to believe in the God of our liturgy and our rituals. A God who created the heavens and the earth and saw that His creation was good, a God who heard the crying of the Israelites in Egypt and parted the Red Sea to free His people from slavery, a God who made a little bit of oil miraculously last for eight days. This was my God, the God I believed in—a God who loved His people, Israel, and performed miracles on their behalf.

But what about here? Why not here? There were no miracles in Auschwitz.

The day it ended for me, the day I can say clearly that my faith died, was Yom Kippur, 1944. Two years earlier on that day, I had watched the German commander of the Radom ammunitions factory make a mockery of the holiest day of the Jewish year, offering up what he called a sacrifice by shooting a good and gentle man to scare us into compliance. Now it was again Yom Kippur, and in the intervening months, more people had been killed than I could tally.

I went outside the barracks soon after we had returned from the morning appel. The sky overhead was smoky black, the air rank with the smell of something rancid and sour. Looking up at that blackness, I knew suddenly that there was no escape for me. Others among us had already been chosen for transport to factories elsewhere in Germany. But I had not been chosen. For me, there would be no exit from this place except through those chimneys. I knew this with certainty: It wasn't a fore-boding or a fear or a premonition. It was knowledge—solid, unshakeable: I would be next, my flesh turned to smoke, my body blackening the sky.

I turned to someone nearby to ask what it was that filled the air with a smell so foul. She told me what she had heard, what people were saying in the camp. She told me matter-of-factly. Why is the sky so black? Why is the smell so bad? Because the Germans are burning the bodies of the Jews and they are collecting the fat that drips from the flesh and they are us-ing it to make soap.

This is what I was told.

Soap.

I had once been given soap in Auschwitz, a coarse, rec-tangular bar with the initials RJF impressed onto it. I didn't know then what the letters stood for, but on that Yom Kippur, someone told me. On Yom Kippur, the day when Jews turn toward their God and seek atonement for their sins, the day when, one prays, God forgives His people and draws near to them in love and reconciliation, on this day, I learned the meaning of RJF—*Rein Juden Fett*, Pure Jewish Fat. They had offered us a cleansing with the corpses of our fellow Jews.

I was seventeen years old. I was a widow and, for all I knew, an orphan as well. I looked into the swelling blackness of that dark, deserted sky; I breathed the putrid, sickening smell of burning human flesh, and I knew that all I had learned, all I had trusted in, all I had believed, was empty, was wrong, a sorrowful lie.

"Where is God? Where is God?" I cried. "If there is a God, why does He not intervene? Now is the time for miracles."

But there were no miracles.

෴

I have envied people their faith. I know some who survived the war and maintained their belief in God, a God of justice and wisdom and mercy. My sons believe, and I am happy for it. They have studied Judaism well, its traditions and its texts, and they are committed to lives bounded by their faith. I marvel to see it, and it makes me proud to watch them in their knowledge and their devotion.

But not me. I cannot muster faith anymore. I wish I could; truly, I wish I could. I think it's easier to live with faith, to believe that in some way, perhaps in a way that surpasses our understanding, justice exists, to believe that there is a God who watches over us and, as our liturgy implores, who hears our voices in prayer. But I do not believe it. I cannot.

Years later, I was listening to a rabbi speak about God. He was talking about God's omnipresence, saying that God is always everywhere—everywhere and at all times aware of the goings-on in the world. To make his point, he said that God was there, too—in the camps, even the death camps of Poland and Germany. How could he say this? Who was he to say this, that God was aware, that God was there? A God who knew and yet did nothing—this was not a God for me. I walked out. I couldn't listen to such a thing.

The only intelligent thing I ever heard a rabbi say about the Holocaust is this: There is no answer; there is no answer to tragedy.

12

TOWARD THE END OF 1944, MIMA AND I WERE TRANSPORTED
one thousand kilometers by sealed boxcar to Lippstadt, Germany, to work at another ammunitions factory. We hadn't
seen my father or Feter or my cousin Moishele since the day
we arrived at Auschwitz six months before. We had no idea
what happened to them. Mima and I were among the last to
leave Auschwitz from our original transport of women from
Radom; there were maybe two hundred of us taken by train to
Germany. On the day we were to leave, we were given some
things: socks—I got one red and one gray—an overcoat
painted on the back with a large yellow X to identify us as prisoners should we try to escape, and, in a final token of utter
insanity, a tablespoon of sugar poured into our palms. We were
told, incredibly, that it was in honor of Hitler's birthday.

Sugar!

People licked it up. I tore a strip from my tattered dress and
carefully poured the grains onto it; I wrapped it up, a neat

package, and held it close, a small stash against the future. I kept my bit of sugar for months: If I felt faint, if I felt I was about to black out, I would unwrap the folded cloth and touch the tip of my tongue to the tiny mound to taste a few grains of something sweet. When we were liberated three months later, I still had a tiny bit of that sugar with me.

From Christmas 1944 until my liberation on April 1, 1945, I worked in Lippstadt. I knew it was Christmastime, because the Hungarian commander of the women at the factory some-how managed to put together a little Christmas scene in the barracks: a bare twig for a tree and a misshapen candle stand-ing beside it. It was heart-breaking, really; I hope it gave her some comfort.

When we first arrived, all the women who had traveled to-gether in the boxcar I was in were put into quarantine. The Germans had heard one of us coughing violently and con-cluded that she must be suffering from typhus. It was a friend of mine, Ruzka Richtman, and all of us knew she was coughing because she had worked in the kuznia in Radom and that breathing the sooty air of the foundry had burned her lungs. We tried to tell the guards that no, it wasn't typhus, that her lungs had been ruined from the kuznia, but they weren't inter-ested in our explanations. So for three weeks, fifty women were made to live in a sealed barracks to wait and see if we would all get sick.

Those weeks were interminable. Mima had been put in a dif-ferent boxcar on the train to Lippstadt, so she wasn't quaran-tined with me. I had lost my partner; I had no one to talk to.

There was nothing to do. We couldn't go outside, we couldn't shower or clean ourselves in any way. Once a day, a guard would open the door of the barracks and hand us something to eat.

We sat. We lay on our bunks. We walked from room to room. There was nothing to do.

I got boils. Large pockets of pus swelled up in the creases of my body, under my arms and in the folds of skin around my groin. I couldn't sit upright for the pain—my thighs pressing on the boils at my groin. When the boils broke and the pus ran out, all I could do was rip off bits of my dress and dab the infected filth with the dirty cloth.

My body was repulsive to me. I was disgusted by myself.

From time to time, the women fought. There was a big argument, I remember, about the sexual status of one of the women. Some women were saying that she was not really a woman, that she wasn't made right, that someone's mother knew someone else who had heard that this woman had gone to Warsaw to get an operation "down there."

"No! It isn't true! I'm married even." She begged the women to stop, to let her be. But they dismissed her, pestered her, mocked her feeble protests. Idle women, scared for their lives, quelling their fears, relieving their boredom through meanness.

Others exchanged recipes—different topic, equally absurd—how many eggs they used in a bobka, how hot to make the oven to get the best crust on a challah.

I didn't understand this, gossiping about scandals, chatting about food. Did these women think that we were going to live? That there would come a time when we would live lives in which a question about the number of eggs you used in a bobka had meaning? It seemed so foreign to me, by this time, that there might actually exist a world somewhere where gossip and idle chatter about food mattered.

To me there was only loneliness, and there was sorrow, and there was death. In those three weeks, I gave up whatever fight I still had in me. I was consumed by my loss of Heniek. I cried for Heniek, and for myself, too. To be honest, I cried for Heniek more than I cried for Mama. I recognized the disparity then, and it pained me, because I loved Mama so very much. But my thoughts were all of Heniek and of the love and passion we had shared. For those few months with him, I had found happiness. I had let myself believe in the future and in promise and possibility. Even in the midst of war, of liquidations and executions and cruelties beyond imagining, I had let myself believe that all was not darkness and death. Heniek had let me believe in life.

Now, for three weeks with nothing to do, alone, with no partner to talk to, my mind turned inward. A thousand times a day, I watched Heniek being led out of the Konzentrationslager, walking away from me, accusing Norembursky of his crime. My mind turned all to death, to the end of everything: Heniek's death, my death. How will I die? How much will it hurt? These thoughts were my companions in quarantine.

After three weeks, when we were finally released—Ruska, of course, did not have typhus, and she survived the war, though just barely—we were taken to the factory in Lippstadt, where for the next ten weeks I worked again making munitions for the Germans. Not much remains with me from this time: I don't remember the exact nature of my work, though I know I got to sit at a machine to do it and that Mima and I were on alternate shifts; she worked nights and I worked days. I don't think I saw Mima even once.

What I remember most clearly from my time in Lippstadt is the remarkable kindness of a German, a man whose name I never knew, whose face I never saw—a man who belonged to the people who sought to destroy me but who, in defiance of his people, offered instead generosity and solace.

He gave me a piece of sandwich.

I always took a little rest when we were given our break between shifts. Just two or three minutes to lay my head down and close my eyes after I had gotten my small portion of soup. This was better to me than trying to get extra soup. When the women would run up and fight each other for the *repeta*—seconds—if it was offered, I would rest instead, lay my head down and sleep, even just for a moment.

One evening, when I picked up my head, I saw a little package wrapped in brown paper lying beside me. I looked at it, but I didn't touch it, because I was worried that someone was testing me, trying to find out if I would take it, only to accuse me of stealing. So I ignored it and went back to my work. The next evening, the same thing happened—a package was left, and I refused to touch it. On the third evening, as I was resting, I suddenly felt a callused hand on my mouth; another hand covered my eyes. A man spoke to me, quietly but urgently. "Don't scream. Don't scream," he said. "I am the one who puts down this package for you. It's me that's leaving you this package."

He was speaking to me in simple German, simple enough for me to understand. He said, "I just want to ask a few questions."

I didn't move, terrified at what this German might want from me.

"Is it true what I am hearing in the underground? Is it true that they are killing Jews? That in Auschwitz they are gassing Jews to death?"

Who was this man assaulting me with his hands on my face? Why was he asking about what the Germans were doing to the Jews?

I didn't trust his tone; I didn't know what to make of the sound of disbelief in his voice. He was a German; he was my enemy. Yet his voice was full of horror as he asked his questions. And he had left something for me, or so he said; he had left me some kind of gift.

He took his hands from my face. I sat motionless, afraid of whatever it was that was happening. I wanted to open the package, but I couldn't bring myself to do it. I couldn't look at him; in all the years of the war—and for years after it, decades—I never looked a German in the eyes.

He tried to calm me; he could see I was terrified. He spoke gently now, still quietly, more plaintive than insistent, trying to convince me that he was on my side. He said, "You can answer me. I am here working in this factory just as you are. I am not out fighting for Hitler. I am against Hitler. Don't be afraid of me. I have been watching you, and I see that you never go for seconds. I thought you might need this more than the others. Here, look, I left this for you from my sandwich."

And he unwrapped the little package himself and showed me what was there: a third of a sandwich, maybe. A piece of salami between slices of brown bread. A feast, this was—meat and bread to bite and chew, meat and bread to be rolled on my tongue, the salt and the fat of it. Two bites, three bites—it was a banquet.

I don't think I had much to tell him. I confirmed, eyes down, lips barely moving, yes, they are gassing people in Auschwitz. But what else did I have to say?

He came every night and gave me a portion of his sandwich. And he came with news, too: that the war would soon be over, that the Americans and the English were on their way, and that the Russians, too, were coming from the other side.

I did believe him about this, because for some weeks already, we could hear the bombs falling not far off. We figured the Allies knew that there were slave-laborers at the factory, because the bombs landed all around, but never in, the factory complex itself. The German civilians must have known, too, because people from the town came to the factory during the raids to hide in the bomb shelters there. The Jews and Russian prisoners, of course, had to stay in the factory as the bombs fell. I told my friend Fela that I wouldn't mind dying in a bomb blast; it would be quick at least, and I suspected it wouldn't hurt too much.

Every night, I took the piece of sandwich and shared it with Fela; she was the girl who some months later would discourage me from spending time with Jack when we were in Garmisch-Partenkirchen. Fela had a little gold ring that she asked me to offer to the German; she wanted to give him something to thank him for the piece of sandwich he was giving me. When I offered it to him, I explained that I was sharing the piece of sandwich with my friend; she and I were partners and shared everything we had. I could tell that he was impressed by this— that I was sharing what little he was able to give me. I know he wished he could have brought more for us to eat, but he said he couldn't bring another sandwich with him to the factory; he was checked by the guards every morning. He wouldn't take the ring. He said we should keep it, in case we might have need of it in the future.

The following evening, when I opened the package, I saw that this man had given me a full half of his sandwich, so there would be more to share. He was now taking less for himself—he was giving up even more—so that I could share his gift with another Jew.

This was astonishing to me, the kindness of this German, the good-heartedness of this man who wanted to do what he could to help two Jews eat. I have thought about this man many times over the years. I am sorry that I was too scared to look at his face; I am sorry that I never asked his name. This man risked his own well-being for my sake—for surely he would have been punished had he been caught giving food to a Jew. Zwirek had extended such goodness two years before; Katz had done so as well. Now, yet another. A Pole, a Jew, and a German: men with kindness harbored in their hearts.

I know that I did not deserve their kindness, any more than I deserved the miseries I was made to suffer. Nothing that happened in the war made sense like that. The world I inhabited was not one in which rewards and punishments were handed out according to reason, according to any standard of justice I could discern. Life and death were the result of happenstance, of luck, of fortune—random events that never added up to anything I could count on.

13

BY THE END OF MARCH 1945, IT WAS AGAIN TIME TO LEAVE. The Germans at the factory apparently knew that the war would soon be over, but they didn't seem to know what to do with us: Lippstadt would fall and they would flee, but they didn't want to leave us behind to work for their victors. The soldiers assigned to the factory floor spent the hours pacing, watching us work; we could almost smell their nervousness. One evening, just before my shift was over, the young officer in charge of our group called us into the yard in front of the factory and told us we were leaving. Immediately. I could tell this was a relief to him, this decision, finally, about how to dispose of us. Instead of returning to the barracks, we were going to walk out of the compound, out of Lippstadt, and head south. The others—like Mima—who were on the night shift were called from their barracks to join us. We wore our frayed, striped dresses and the old coats we still had with us from Auschwitz.

The last time I had been on such a march, eight months earlier, we had walked from Radom to Tomaszów, in the scorching heat of high summer. Now, in late March, the weather was still wintry, especially at night, and the road was stiff with frozen mud and ice. We walked pressed against each other to shield ourselves from the cold. We were a long and weary column, perhaps two hundred of us in all, flanked on either side by our still-anxious German guards, clutching the guns slung across their chests, their heavy boots crunching in the ice. We walked for two nights in the wicked winter cold, not knowing where we were being led or what the Germans would do with us. During the days, we were hidden from sight—once, I remember, in an abandoned barn filled with hay. I thought the Germans were locking us in to set fire to the place; I thought we were about to be burned alive. I waited a long time in that barn, straining to hear the first crack of flame.

Then, on the third morning of the march, it ended. Literally out of nowhere, out of an otherwise empty sky. It was very early, just before dawn, and the air had that feeling of freshness that can sometimes emerge in the moments when night seems ready to give over into day. I was chilled, and I clutched my coat at the collar to try to keep off the dampness of the air. Mima was walking beside me, our arms nearly touching for the warmth. We were very tired, exhausted really, after another long, dark night of walking—after so many years of war. I could tell we weren't far from a town—Kaunitz, as it turned out—because the road had gotten firmer under our feet and I thought I could see lights quivering in the distance. People were getting up with the dawn, readying themselves for another day.

Then we heard the rumble of airplanes, a muffled roar approaching in the brightening light of a gunmetal sky.

As if in response to some silent command, the guards started to shout at us all at once: "Get down! Everyone, on your bellies. Faces down!" A sudden eruption of activity broke the monotony of our endless walk. The soldiers, unslinging their guns, ran to surround us as we fell to the ground. Someone yelled out the order again: "No moving! Don't lift your heads!" I dug my face into the frozen dirt, certain the Germans would shoot. I could feel Mima next to me, but I was too scared to inch my way over to find her hand. I did as I was told: I lay still; I didn't move my head. Above us now, the boom of airplanes roaring by; around us, the anxious breath of the soldiers stamping their feet in the cold. Did it last an hour? Maybe just ten minutes. I don't know.

Then shooting began. Not at us, but not too far away—down the road some small distance—we heard the rapid crack of gunfire. "We're next. We're next," I kept thinking. "Now is when I'm going to die." I had decided that it would be worse than a bomb blast, that it would take longer to die from a gunshot. I didn't want to die slowly; I didn't want to die in pain. I breathed in the dirt, bits of grit flecking my frozen lips. I kept my eyes tightly shut. I tried to ready myself for the bullets.

Sometime later, we heard that it was another group of women who had left the factory with us—a group of Russian prisoners—that had been shot. They had been walking ahead of us, and they, too, had been ordered to get down as the sound of the planes approached, and then the Germans shot them, every one of them, right on the road. Apparently, this little massacre led to our liberation—because just as the Russians were being shot, the Americans were flying overhead, and when they saw what was happening below—women being shot in the back—they decided to intervene. So down they came in parachutes—dozens of them, falling from the sky. We had the impression that they didn't have prior orders for this, that it wasn't planned, because when Mima said it was safe to look up, to lift my head from the dirt (a thing I didn't want to do; I didn't believe—I couldn't believe—that the Germans had fled), I saw soldiers, American soldiers, falling randomly from the sky, and some of them were bloodied from their fall, some had landed on the fences by the side of the road, their parachutes caught in the wooden posts. One young soldier I saw was dangling from the limbs of a tree. But Mima was right—it was safe to lift our heads, because the Germans had run away. We arose, dazed and disbelieving, and found ourselves surrounded only by Americans, young men talking in a language we didn't understand but telling us news we did. It was over: The Germans were gone; we were free.

They had been standing above us just moments before, their guns pointed at our backs, readying themselves to shoot. But then, instead of shooting, they ran. It was only a minute, a second, that separated my life from my death. I could have been dead; I was about to be dead. But, instead—I don't know why—I was alive.

The edge between life and death is so sharp, so arbitrary, so senseless.

Liberation was a bewilderment to me. I remember throwing aside the little packet of sugar I still had with me from

Auschwitz, thinking suddenly that I wouldn't need it any-more. I remember thinking—no, I remember knowing, with clarity—that I no longer wanted to be a Jew, that I wanted simply to be a human being without the encumbrances of history and obligation. And I remember a sudden fright, a terrifying question rising up in me from the hollow of my gut: To whom do I belong, and who belongs to me?

I had Mima: I know that; I knew it then. Still, I had lost what mattered most: my mother, my Heniek. Standing amid exuberance, amid tears of thankfulness and disbelieving smiles, I was shaken by a wrenching awareness: I was free, I would have a future, but I would enter it alone.

14

IN THE SEVERAL MONTHS BEFORE JACK DIED—IN 2006, AT the age of ninety-two—his thoughts often returned to our time together in Garmisch-Partenkirchen. Jack loved me very much—I say this with simple candor—and I know it gave him pleasure to see me well dressed and well fed, to see me surrounded by beautiful things. We started together from nothing; once our real estate business became successful, he wanted to see that I should always have everything. He called me his queen. From the start and even into our old age, he said that the world was envious that he walked with me on his arm. But in the end—at the end—what mattered most to him was that I had come to his doorstep in 1945.

"I cannot believe that you came to me, that you came looking for me. I am not a believer, Millie, but I believe God sent you to find me."

He was thinking of Garmisch-Partenkirchen.

Jack, too, had been alone in the world. Except for his brother Mannes, who had moved to New York before World War I and whom Jack had never met, all of Jack's siblings—there had been eight children in all—were gone. Some had died before the war; some were killed during it. Most of his cousins were killed as well, as were nearly all of his nieces and nephews, and his father and grandparents, too—his mother had died when he was a young child. His wife, Rachel, to whom he had been married for just three or four years when he was arrested, and his little daughter, Emma, were both gone. A flourishing, thriving family, all now dead. At the edge of despair, Jack had managed to find purpose and a will to live in his efforts to help save nearly seven hundred boys who had come in a transport to Buchenwald in the summer of 1944. After the war, Jack eventually found his way to Garmisch-Partenkirchen, and he moved in with one of his cousins who had survived—Itamar, who was living in that apartment he shared with the group of other Radomers.

Jack had been in Garmisch for several weeks when I arrived late in the summer of 1945. Like an angel out of the wilderness, a harbinger of happiness, I came. That is how Jack saw it—or, that is how he wanted to remember it, that in all the world, I managed to come searching for him, to raise up his soul from the devastation of the war. In the final weeks of his life, that memory rose up again and lingered with him. In those last weeks, he mentioned it often.

෴

It wasn't true, exactly, that I had come to Garmisch-Partenkirchen looking for Jack. Mima and I had come because we were looking for Radomers, and when Mima wanted to move on, when she wanted to go to Italy because she had heard that her husband and her brother-in-law—my father— were in Bari waiting for a boat to Palestine, she left me with Jack or, at least, in Jack's protection. She said simply: "You'll be safe with Jack."

I did feel safe with Jack. I was riveted by his stories, by the enormity of his hardships, by his determination to get through it all. He was so smart and so strategic in his dealings with his captors—figuring out exactly which rocks were best to pick up, or working out where exactly to hide the many children in his charge so the Germans wouldn't find them. I admired him for this, and I pitied him, too, for the horrors he had endured—hanging for hours by his upturned arms from a gallows, being whipped on his naked back until he fainted from the pain, being buried once under corpses and rescued only by happenstance. Compared with his, my own stories to me seemed insignificant. Maybe, knowing that he could go on and envision a future for himself despite his past helped me to see that perhaps I could, too.

Jack had lost his wife and child, as I had lost my Heniek. We spoke about this, at least a little. I could never bring myself to tell Jack everything about my feelings for Heniek—and why should I, really? He didn't need to know all the details, just as I didn't need to know every detail about his wife. But talking to each other about even the outlines of our previous loves brought us closer together. Honesty does that.

Still, though, I was certain I wouldn't marry again, and I told Jack so. That, too, surprisingly perhaps, brought us closer to each other, perhaps because it made Jack pursue me with more persistence, but also I think because knowing I wouldn't marry him, and so knowing that nothing really was at stake, allowed me to feel comfortable with him. It made me feel safe, for the first time in years.

My determination not to remarry slowly faded, imperceptibly almost, over the several months I spent in Garmisch-Partenkirchen. I found myself seeking out Jack's company. So after many hours of quiet conversation, when he sat, twirling that ring between his fingers, asking, "Whose finger will this fit?" I found myself suspecting that it would fit mine.

We decided to go together to Italy.

By this time, Mima had been away for weeks and we hadn't heard anything back from her or from anyone who had seen her. I wanted to find out what happened and whether she had found Feter and my father. This is how it was after the war— Jews traipsing all over Europe, jumping on trains, sleeping in abandoned buildings, trying to find anyone in their family who might still be alive. As it turned out, Feter and my father had been told that Mima and I had been killed in Auschwitz; a woman they knew from Radom had told them that she had seen us going to the gas chambers. So they had gone to Bari, where they heard you could get smuggled to Palestine. Mima wound up finding them there, in Bari, but the meeting brought relief and devastation at once. Mima learned then that although Feter had survived, their son, Moishele, had not. She had seen Moishele last when the men were taken away at Auschwitz, and all the time since then she had been hoping, praying, that Feter might have been able to protect him, to save him from the gas chambers.

Mima and Moishele before the war

I don't think Mima ever recovered from what she learned that day in Italy. None of us recovered, really, from the war—it's an absurdity, a way of not wanting to deal with things, to pretend otherwise. But Mima had held her hope for Moishele so close to her heart—I think maybe all the time she was protecting me, there was some part of her hoping that Feter was doing the same for their son. But Feter hadn't been able to protect him.

Did she blame him? I wonder. Did something in her love for Feter die on the day she learned of Moishele's death? Chava had been killed in Feter's care; now Mima learned that Moishele had, too. In truth, there's nothing Feter could have

Mima and me, 1946

done to save his children, but the heart doesn't always abide by such truths. Mima had helped me survive; her own children perished. Mima and Feter never had another child, though Mima was only in her early thirties when the war ended. She was sad, I think, all her days.

Jack and I, of course, knew nothing of this at the time, so we decided to make the trip to Italy to search for Mima and any family she might have found. In the end, we didn't find our family in Italy. Mima, Feter, and my father were returning to Garmisch-Partenkirchen just as we were making our way south, and it was only after we finally got back to Germany that we were all united. But our trip through Italy turned out to be perilous in ways we couldn't have imagined, and the experience of it bound Jack and me to each other. When we returned, I was wearing Jack's ring.

We traveled to Italy by train, and to be honest, it was a fairly festive time. We carried with us Displaced Person cards, which allowed us passage on any train, and Jack had accumulated a little pocket money by selling cigarettes and other small items in Garmisch, so we were able to buy a little food—perhaps a sandwich to share—along the way. With us on the train to Florence, which was our first stop, was a group of Italian soldiers returning home from Russian POW camps. They were joyous in their liberation, and we spent the hours listening to them sing Italian classics. It was late fall in Italy. The weather was crisp and bright, the air smelled fresh, the soldiers were drunk with the anticipation of home, and I was traveling with a man I found myself starting to love. The soldiers gave us bread and wine, and we ate and drank and listened to their full-throated songs. It was good, all of this; it was good. It felt like life.

In Florence, we found a cousin who told us that Mima had gone south. We decided to continue south, too, hoping to meet up with her en route or to find her in Bari. We spent the night in Florence, at a little hotel near the train station. Though it cost us more money than we wanted to spend, we took two rooms; I was given a room on the first floor, and Jack got one all the way up on the sixth or seventh. Before we parted for the night, I remember, Jack stood at the top of the winding staircase in the center of the main hall; he waved down to me, sending me good-night wishes, and I looked all the way up and waved back. Such a simple pleasure that was— waving softly toward a loving face looking sweetly down. It made me laugh, that silly scene, and I realized suddenly that I was having fun. I hadn't thought it was possible.

In the morning, we set off for Livorno, which we intended to be just a stopping-off point on our way to Bari. But while we were there, we somehow found out that Mima had found Feter and my father in Bari and that they were already on their way north, back to Germany. So we turned around. We looked for a place to spend the night, but all we found were buildings marked *albergo*, which is how you say "hotel" in Italian, but we didn't know that at the time. We thought there was no place for us to sleep. Still, Jack said not to worry, he would figure something out.

He had a pocketknife with him, and with it he cut several branches from a palm tree and laid them out next to a building close to the train station. "This will be our bed," he said, "here, under the stars." I was nervous about sleeping outside, on a street by the station, which is never the nicest part of any town. But Jack was confident; he seemed so sure of himself, and he always had a little joke to ease my mind.

"Don't worry, Maniusia. No one will steal our diamonds."

Of course, we had no diamonds.

"Here," he said, "lie down next to me."

He made a place for me on a bed of palms. I curled myself next to him and let myself relax into his protective care.

He wrapped his arms around me to keep me warm. He whispered to me then, gently, softly, "I know I am much older than you, but if I am not too old, if you will have me, I would want very much to marry you." And he reached into his pocket and held out to me the ring he had been playing with back in Garmisch-Partenkirchen.

I had known, I suppose, that we were headed toward marriage, once I agreed to travel with him to Italy. And Jack was so persistent in his pursuit, so single-minded in his evident devotion, he was rather hard to resist. He thought of me, I think, almost as a child—young and lovely and in some way unspoiled despite my experience—and I think that just as he had found life and life-giving purpose in helping to protect the transport of children brought to Buchenwald, so he found it enlivening to protect and care for me. I came to him out of the wilderness, a young thing in need of nurture. I accepted this role; I even embraced it, for I wanted someone older and wiser in the ways of the world. I wanted someone to be strong where I felt weak, someone determined to find joy where I was so prone now to find only sadness and emptiness.

I did not let go of Heniek. First love is so pure, so uncompromised by the demands and details of life. That joy—

Heniek loves me! He chose me!—it doesn't go away. But it can get put away, to make way for other things. So although I didn't let go of my love for Heniek, I did let go of my determination never to marry again. I opened myself—I opened my heart—to Jack.

I said yes.

We spent the night half-awake, nervously watching all about us. But I was wrapped in Jack's arms, and I felt safe.

We began our journey home.

We found the train back toward Germany. It was quiet in the train, with only a few people, and quite without any boisterous singing. At the Austrian border, officials came to check papers. We had the same Displaced Person cards we carried on the way down, but though they had been sufficient then, for some reason—we couldn't understand what the Italian guards were saying; we didn't know what was wrong—they were deemed insufficient now. So again, after everything, after allowing ourselves to believe that it was all over, that we were done with soldiers and guns and orders called out in unremitting anger—again, we were arrested, taken away at gunpoint, and thrown into a jail.

The place was pitch-black and cold. We were locked in a small room of some kind, without windows or ventilation; we couldn't get our bearings, because it was so dark. I could sense that there were two others in the room, but they must have been as frightened as we were, because no one said a word. It seemed so long in that darkness. Slowly, our eyes began to grow accustomed to the dark, and I could begin to make out the contour of two faces, and eyes glinting like the eyes of cats pointed in our direction.

"Mania! It's us, Mania and Alter Singer!"

Unbelievable. Incredible. We had been thrown into a cell with a couple who had been brought to the Radom factory during the war. Mania and I had slept in the same barracks. It was an inexplicable coincidence, yet, I suppose, no more inexplicable than anything else we had been through.

We fell upon each other as if we each had found a lost treasure: a known face, a lingering embrace, a remnant of home.

After a day or so, we were taken from the jail to a refugee camp of some kind. Though it didn't seem well guarded— there were no watchtowers, no Germans manhandling us with batons or machine guns—the camp, surrounded by barbed wire and filled with throngs of frightened men and women, still too closely resembled the places we had so recently been freed from for us to trust that nothing bad would happen to us there.

One day after we arrived, we lifted up a piece of fence, crawled underneath, and set ourselves free. No one seemed to notice.

The four of us started to walk north, toward the Alps.

We met up with a small band of Jewish smugglers. They were headed toward Austria, and they agreed to take us with them as long as we were able to keep up with them on our own; they told us they wouldn't wait for us if our pace slowed. They knew their way across the Alps, and we could follow along in their tracks—it was November or December by this time, and the mountains were high with snow—but they had

to be across the border by morning and they simply would not
wait for anything.

We were unprepared for such a journey. Neither Jack nor I
had ever hiked in the mountains; we came from Radom, after
all, an industrial city with barely a hill, let alone a mountain,
and we had spent the past half-decade fending off starvation.
We weren't built for such a trek. We had come to Italy by
train, and we assumed we would return the same way. I had a
sweater and pants made from a soldier's uniform so I at least
had clothes that had some thickness to them, some strength.
But Jack was wearing just a simple suit—a suit for the city, not
something to wear trekking over mountains in the cold of
winter. And we didn't have the proper shoes: You need boots
to climb a mountain, and boots we didn't have. Nor gloves.

Still, we were grateful to have guides. We set off.

First, I remember, we had to cross a river. The air was icy
cold, the water was colder still, and the river was running fast.
It was night, too, and it was hard to see where we were going.
The Alters were ahead of us; the smugglers, our guides, were
ahead of them. Jack and I held on to each other, struggling
against the strong push of the current. We were unused to
such effort. Our muscles began to seize, tight and taut as rope,
cramping from the strain.

We made it across—a miracle it was—but Jack at some
point had hurt his knee and our pace soon slowed. We became
separated from our friends and our guides. We were somewhere
in the Alps, nearing the onset of winter, in the depths of the
night. And we were alone and had no idea where to go.

Up. Where else could we go? We went up, up toward the
peak of the mountain so we could get down to the other side.

The absurdity of it! The two of us, without food or water, mountain climbing without guides, without light, without proper clothes. But what choice did we have? There was nothing to do but go up, nothing to do but climb.

So we climbed. Throughout the night, in snow that reached up almost to our knees, each step an effort beyond what we could reasonably accomplish. We kept thinking we must be nearing the crest, we must be getting close, but ahead of us always was just more mountain, more and more steps reaching up.

We were very cold, we were very tired, and we started to become very scared.

At some point, we reached a plateau and sat down on the snow to rest. I heard the howl of animals. Mountain leopards, I thought, maybe jackals. The sound of hungry animals must have been there before, but I hadn't paid any attention as I walked; I must have been concentrating only on being able to take the next step. But now, huddled against Jack in cold that could shatter stone, I could hear the howl of beasts echoing in the predawn light.

I knew we couldn't stay there. If we sat still much longer, if we happened to fall asleep, we might freeze to death. And I feared the animals would come upon us as we slept and would eat us alive. Jack wanted to stay, to rest a while longer from our trek. He joked about my fear: "Maybe the animals, at least, will get breakfast." He was just as scared as I was, I knew that, but somehow he could always turn things into a joke. Maybe that was his protection, the jokes his shield against the fear.

I told Jack that we had to leave, or we would die all alone in the mountains and no one would find us.

It was starting now to become light, and we spotted through the trees a small house in the far distance, all the way down the mountain. A cottage, we thought, where perhaps we might find a moment's shelter, a little warmth, maybe even a drop of food. It was very far down, the mountain was very steep, and Jack was afraid to move. But I refused to stay. I feared the cold and, even more, the howling of the animals.

We walked to the edge of the plateau, sat down with our legs outstretched—me in front, Jack straddling me from behind—like a toboggan, the two of us, a two-man sled in the snow. We pushed off and started down the slope.

It seemed to work for a while, sliding down the mountain together toward that light in the distance. But soon we were going too fast. Beneath the top layer of snow was a thicker, deeper layer of ice. As we slid, we could feel its hardness against our backsides, little juts tearing into the fabric of our clothes, cutting through our pants but not slowing our descent. We were racing down an icy mountain slope, and we had no way to steer or stop.

As we neared the tree line, I noticed a thick tree stump jutting out from the snow in front of us. I reached out with my leg and managed, somehow—I don't know how—to hook my foot against it, which abruptly stopped our fall. We crashed, tumbling on top of each other in the snow. But we broke no bones.

We picked ourselves up and walked the rest of the way, grabbing on to the tree trunks and branches for support as we made our way down.

The cottage was old and shabby. We knocked quietly on the thin wooden door, not wanting to wake everyone inside.

An old man answered, thin and stooped; we could see just past him into the one small room: A cow stood idly in the middle. The man had no barn for his animal, so it lived with him. We knew this man couldn't have much, but we were fairly desperate. We hadn't eaten in two days; we had been sucking on bits of ice. I took off my ring, the little band Jack had given to me just a few days earlier in Livorno, and held it out to him. We had nothing else to offer, and we needed, desperately, to eat. But the man wouldn't take it. He told us, in German, that we were now in Austria—we had managed to cross the border without knowing it—but that he had nothing he could give us; he could barely feed his own family with the meager amount he had.

He wished us luck and sent us on our way.

It was full daylight by this time, and we were worried that we might be taken for smugglers in this border town. We must have looked a mess after our night on the mountain. We fell in with a group of workers and tried to walk along with them so we would not be noticed. I walked behind Jack, keeping my eyes down, wanting, as ever, to be unseen. But I saw. Looking down, I saw that Jack's pants, flimsy city things unfit for the mountains, had been torn to shreds on the ice, and as they tore, his skin tore, too, and now the shreds of fabric and skin had frozen together. His backside was frozen—threads and flesh and blood—frozen into one. He must have been too cold, perhaps too scared, to feel the pain. I knew we had to get inside somewhere; he had to warm his body. What would happen if he got frostbite on his backside?

We passed a store; maybe it was a bakery, I don't know. I remember there were round ovens inside. We went in and showed the woman there what had happened to Jack—he just turned around and I pointed to his backside. She let us warm up by the ovens, and she gave me a needle and thread to try to sew up Jack's pants after they had softened and I was able delicately to separate the fabric from his skin. It wasn't very good; the pants really needed a big patch, but we managed. As always, we managed.

We found our way to the train station and headed, without event—thank God—back to Germany.

In later years, Jack and I would marvel at what we went through on our little adventure in Italy. How stupid we were to try to cross the Alps on our own—two city-dwellers tackling a mountain. It's absurd, if you think about it even for a moment. We could have died out there on the mountains, and no one would ever have known. But somehow, by luck, by chance, by nothing more solid than that—somehow we made it, and when we arrived back in Garmisch-Partenkirchen, we made our arrangements to get married.

15

JACK WAS A ROMANTIC. FROM THE VERY BEGINNING UNTIL the very end, he always wanted to sweep me off my feet, to celebrate my presence in his life. We were married on January 24, 1946. We had no money, no photographer, few guests. The war was still raw for all of us, and we were all as much aware of the many, many people who weren't with us as we were of those few people who were. Weddings in those days weren't simply joyous affairs. But Jack worked hard to make the day grand, and I loved him for the ardor of his effort.

I was finally reunited with my father when Jack and I returned to Garmisch-Partenkirchen. My father agreed, heartily, to the marriage: Jack was known to be a good man, and he came from a good family. Feter gladly endorsed the idea, too. Feter's approval mattered a lot to me; during the war, he had saved my life. Twice, really—first, when he had

My father, several months after the war

forced me, against my will, to go to the factory to work, and then again when he figured out where to hide me during the oblava in the factory kitchen. He had protected me during the war; his opinion of what I should do afterward meant a lot to me.

I went to the rabbi in town to ask him to perform the *chuppah*. I didn't mind so much one way or the other whether a rabbi would officiate at the wedding; I was done with all that, and had been since Auschwitz. I went to the rabbi out of respect for my father and uncle; I knew they would care, and I wanted to please them. But I suppose there are times—not many, perhaps, but a few over the course of my life—when my own sense of what is right has outweighed my tendency to conform to other people's pleasures. This was one of those times.

The rabbi was an elderly man with watery eyes and vague wisps of a beard. He looked every inch the part, and he spoke to me with a distant formality as we sat across from each other at a table in the apartment where he lived. There was simply no softness in the man. Perhaps he had seen too much during the war; perhaps he had been through too much himself. I know he, too, had survived the camps. What was left of him—if there ever had been any more—was hardened, as unfeeling as stone. He agreed to officiate at the wedding, but told me that first I had to go to the *mikveh*, to be ritually purified, according to tradition.

This struck me as outrageous. Purified? Me? In what way, precisely, had I been sullied? I asked him, "Rabbi, do you know where I have been? I have just come from Auschwitz, and you want me to go to the mikveh?"

He didn't care. What mattered to him were only the exacting details of the law. He insisted: Either I go to the mikveh, or he would refuse to perform the wedding.

"Would you prefer that I live with a man without a chuppah? Is that better?" I asked.

I thought perhaps he might try to convince me, might try to explain to me the importance of going to the mikveh. Maybe he understood the meaning of this ritual; he was a rabbi, after all. Maybe he understood what made it necessary for me to be "purified" before I was wed.

But he wasn't interested in conversation or explanation. He nearly spat at me: "I don't care what you do: Either you go to the mikveh, or I won't perform the chuppah."

So I shot back, suddenly, uncharacteristically, defiant: "Then you are not the rabbi for me." I got up, turned around, and walked out.

I was so proud of that! It felt so good. Even now, when I think about it, I am proud that I had the courage to stand up to that man. For years already, people had been telling me what to do. They said, "Go," I went; they said, "Work," I worked. "Get up"; "Lie down"; "Stand here"; "Go there." That was my life; I had been formed within the pattern of being obedient to orders. But when I went to this rabbi, hardened and hard-hearted as he was, something in me suddenly stood up to protest. His unconsidered command hit up against something solid in me, something strong and unbending, something that said, simply, "No. I won't do this. It makes no sense." It was my small bid to right an infinitely skewed world. And it felt good.

Jack didn't mind; maybe he was even a little bit proud of me, too. Instead, my uncle would perform the wedding. He had married me to Heniek in the ghetto; he would marry me to Jack, now.

Jack made all the arrangements, such as they were. He had been buying whiskey in Stuttgart, where it was cheaper, and selling it in Lippstadt for a small profit, so he had accumulated a little money. He bought burgundy-colored material, which we had made into a wedding dress. The dressmaker asked to be paid in food, so Jack asked Srulik Rosensweig, the man who worked in the American kitchen and would bring cans of soup for us back to the apartment, to take something from the kitchen to pay the dressmaker, and he did. Jack wanted me to have my hair done, like a proper, elegant lady. So he found a hairdresser and went out and scavenged some wood so she could build a fire to heat the water she washed my hair with. He asked my father to go to Feldafing, a deportation camp not far from Munich, to see if he could find some kosher meat to serve at our little wedding party. We were living like vagabonds with nearly nothing to our names, managing from day to day on leftovers, scraps, whatever bits and pieces we could find—a sandwich made from the fat off the top of a can of soup; a dress stitched together from a soldier's discarded uniform. And yet Jack took these bits and pieces and out of them created a miracle of a day, a wonder of a wedding.

He gave me chrysanthemums. A cold-weather flower, a flower needing long nights to bloom, a flower befitting our experience. But these chrysanthemums were white and lush and thick with life, befitting the day.

Jack took me to the attic of the apartment—he always thought attics held a special romance; he offered me the flowers, and he gave me a scrap of paper torn from a brown bag on which he had written a wedding poem:

בלומען ווייסע בלומען צארטע

ווי דיין נשמה ריין פון זינד

טראץ דאס שווערע לעבן דאס הארטע

נישט פערענדערט פון שטורם און ווינד

די צארטע בלומען וואס איך דיר היינט שיק

זאלן אויך ווייטער דיין סימבאל זיין

מיין ווינטש פון טיפן הארצן שטראלט פון ליבע גליק

איך זאל דער לעצטער אין די מיין לעצטע בלייבן מיין

White flowers, tender flowers
Like your soul free from sin
Despite the difficult, hard life
Not altered by storm, cold and wind.

The tender flowers I send to you today
May they continue to be your symbol;
From the depth of my heart
My wish beams with love and much joy
I should be your last one and you my last one,
Always mine.

In the middle of winter, a flowering poem, a poem like a flower that grows white, despite its sojourn in the dark.

208

After all that Jack had endured, where did he find the resources to write something of such delicate beauty? This was astonishing to me. And, too, the hopeful confidence about the future without pretending to eclipse the past—that we were not for each other the first, but, oh, that we might be for each other the last. I treasure this poem, its beauty, its honesty, its love.

I read the poem with Jack looking on. When I was done and looked up at him, overcome, I think, by the simple beauty of the thing in my hands, Jack took me in his arms and bent his head to mine, and he kissed me then with a passion, an urgency even, I had not known he owned. And I was surprised to find and pleased—relieved, to be true—that I wanted him just as much. I wanted him, too.

We went first to a German justice of the peace for a civil ceremony. Jack joked, "I'm taking you to a priest to get married." It was, I have to say, somewhat mortifying to stand before a German official and listen to him pronounce us man and wife. What had the man been doing a year earlier? Where had he been? But never mind. It was a bright winter day, and we rode to City Hall in an open sleigh drawn by a white horse. It was something out of a fairy tale—me in my new wedding dress holding my oh-so-white flowers and the snow glistening all around. It was beautiful, and it was fresh and clean and crisply bright.

My uncle performed the chuppah at the apartment. Other than the two of us, my father, Mima, and Feter—we had maybe twelve other people with us, all from Radom. The ceremony was performed according to tradition; the celebration after, with meat supplied by my father, was simple and brief. A friend of ours somehow managed to scrounge two oranges for the occasion—a rare delicacy even before the war. Those oranges provided what luxury the wedding had, and we were grateful to see them set on our wedding table.

It wasn't much, but it was enough. Jack and I had found each other. We were in love. We were married. That was a start. That was enough.

Jack and me, 1946

16

JACK HAD NEVER MET HIS BROTHER MANNES, AND I COULD tell that my husband was both eager and anxious when we arrived at the door of Mannes's handsome Victorian home in Beacon, New York. It was the end of June 1946; we had been met at the boat by Jack's uncle Philip, and he had brought us up the Hudson Valley that first evening to stay with Mannes, who had guaranteed our passage. The door opened on an elegant entryway, and we saw Jack's brother and his wife standing in the gentle light. Mannes stepped forward at once, greeting us warmly, enfolding us both in an oversized embrace.

Mannes's wife, Brina, on the other hand, was another story entirely. She stood stiffly beside him, arms folded across her ample chest. We were ushered into the front hall; she said a formal hello to Jack, and then, glancing briefly up and down the length of me, she asked Jack, "This is your wife?" She didn't address me; she didn't extend a hand; she barely nodded in my direction. As if I were some appendage, like a piece of old luggage Jack had brought along.

Then, to me, for the first time: "You should take a bath." Not "Please come in. You must be tired from your trip. Would you like to sit down?" Not "Would you like something to drink?" Not "Welcome to my home. Thank God you have survived and made it to America." Not anything warm, not anything human. Just "Take a bath," as if before she could touch me, before she could sanction my body on her bedsheets, she needed first to ensure that I washed the European germs off me.

Okay, I thought, okay. Maybe I'm being a little sensitive; maybe I'm mishearing the iciness, the cold condescension in her voice. She was, after all, a rich and well-established woman. Her husband had invented the design for one-piece pilot uniforms. Like the children's snowsuits you see now, where a single zipper extends from one shoulder all the way across the body and down the opposite leg, the design had allowed airmen to get into and out of their uniforms with ease. Mannes had gotten multiple military contracts during the war and had grown rich. Brina was from Radom, just like the rest of us, but she was a big shot in America now, and here I was, fresh from an overseas voyage out of an old and old-fashioned world. She probably saw me gaping at the Studebaker in the driveway as I came in; who had ever seen anything like that before? Maybe what I heard as dismissive disdain was just a newfangled form of formality.

I took my few things and went upstairs. As I undressed in the attic bedroom where we would sleep, I heard the tub being filled on the second floor, which surprised me, because I thought I would be expected to draw my own bath, especially given the way I had been treated when I first arrived. I went down to the bathroom and slipped into the warmth of the tub. That was good. It was good to let myself relax, to settle down into the suds. I was newly pregnant by this time and had just spent ten days on rocky seas lying nauseous on a bunk in the lower deck of an army transport boat.

Someone knocked at the door. "Don't wash your face." It was Mannes. I couldn't understand why he would say that, but I didn't pay it much attention. A few minutes later, he knocked again. And again came the obscure instruction through the door: "Malka"—he called me by my Yiddish name—"don't wash your face with the bathwater." This got me nervous, wondering what was wrong with the water that I shouldn't let it touch my face. Then a third time: "Don't wash your face, Malka. We put a disinfectant in the water."

It was like the earth had opened underneath me. I was back in Auschwitz, being deloused. I had thought that, finally, I had arrived in a place of safety, a place where I wouldn't have to feel myself always the outsider, the unwanted, the scum of the earth. I had thought that maybe here, in this new land of opportunity, Jack and I could start again from scratch, start clean and build something together, a new life. But I was made to realize that here it was no different; here, even in my own family, I was still the dirty Jew.

I hadn't wanted to come to America. Even though Jack wanted very much to meet his one remaining sibling, I kept thinking of what my grandfather said to me when I was a

On the boat to America

child—that the streets in America were made from traif. Even with all the optimism people had after the war for the endless opportunities of America—in America you could be anything, in America people could grow rich—still, America seemed frighteningly foreign to me, utterly unlike anything I understood as home. But I knew that I didn't have a home in Europe anymore. A couple Jack knew had returned to Radom some months after the war, and they had been hanged by the local Poles, who presumably feared that the couple might want their property back. So Jack worked with the Hebrew Immigrant Aid Society, the Jewish agency in Europe, to arrange for our passage, and we set off, along with my father and Jack's one remaining nephew, Sidney, in the middle of June 1946.

It had started out well enough. We recognized Jack's uncle, Philip, at the docks because he was carrying a sign that said "Werber" on it, and we pushed our way through the throng to get to him. Philip took us first to his apartment in the Bronx. He told us he was a roofer and showed us all the roofs along the Grand Concourse that he had worked on. The Grand Concourse in those days was a fancy area; the men dressed in fur collars and the women wore sheer stockings made of nylon. We thought he must be a millionaire to have made all those roofs, but as it turned out, he only fixed roofs; he didn't lay them from scratch. Still, his apartment building was on a lovely, tree-lined street, and as we entered his apartment, we saw a tremendous table that seemed to stretch the length of the entire living room. It was piled with food. We couldn't believe how much food—roasted chicken, sliced brisket, potatoes steaming hot in a porcelain bowl. We had never eaten such a feast. We thought, this is what America is, this profusion, this easy availability of luxury. Jack's uncle, a simple roof-fixer from Poland, had his own apartment and didn't want for food; he even owned a car. It felt good to get to this America. This land of possibility, we thought, might hold possibility for us, too.

That seemed less true—or not even true at all—once we arrived at Mannes's house. For the three weeks we spent there, we were made to feel that we were nothing at all.

I had brought with me from Europe a bar of soap, a little oval of Palmolive soap that smelled like a field of fresh-cut flowers. Mima had found it somewhere when we were living in Kaunitz. This bar of soap, neatly wrapped in its corrugated green paper, was for me a token of another world, long before the war, a world where women had soft skin and silken hair, a world in which women could walk down the street and smell fresh and clean—like the women from the magazines my mother used to keep in our apartment for her clients to look at. I loved this little bar of soap, and I decided right away when Mima gave it to me that I would never use it; I didn't want to use it up with water and washing. I made myself a little promise instead—that whenever I would be able to buy real underwear, whenever I could get some panties and bras and stockings of my own, I would nestle this sweet-smelling bar of soap among my delicate underthings, and I would be able to wear that lovely scent upon me every day.

And that's what I did. I kept the soap as a sachet, and when I arrived in Beacon fourteen months later, I still had that bar of soap with me.

After ten or twelve days on the boat, and now in Beacon for several more, I wanted to do some clothes washing, so I asked Brina if there was someplace I could wash out a few of our clothes. Yes, she said, in the basement; I could find a basin and a slop sink there, but she didn't have any soap. "Oh, I have some soap," I told her. "I'll give you mine." Though I thought it was odd that she didn't have any soap for her own washing, I went and got my bar of Palmolive, and Brina took it from me and ripped off the paper wrapping, and, handing it back to me, said, "Good, you can use this."

So I washed out our clothes in the basement slop sink, and I used up my little bar of soap. I gently cried the whole time as I watched it dissolve.

When Mannes saw me later that day, he could tell that I had been crying, even though I tried to hide it. He asked what was wrong. I told him I was fine, that I had just been doing some washing during the afternoon and I was tired. He asked if I liked the washing machine they had. Washing machine? What washing machine? I did everything by hand. "Why did you do that, Malka? We have a beautiful machine that will do the washing for you." And he showed me the thing in the basement, and he pointed out the box of soap powder on the shelf right above it. It was Ivory soap. I didn't know the name, and I couldn't read the English writing on the box.

Why was Brina so harsh? She didn't know me; she didn't know Jack. What could she possibly have had against us that she treated me with such contempt?

Perhaps I was an embarrassment to her; perhaps she thought of me as the immigrant Polish servant girl. I was prost, common, like Chava, Chiel Friedman's wife. Brina treated me as the ignorant laborer, alive only to do her bidding.

Mannes suggested that Brina take me shopping. I had been wearing a suit I had made in Europe using material from a suit that belonged to a man. It had a loose-fitting jacket and a long, wide skirt. It wasn't much, but I thought it was pretty enough. Apparently, though, it wasn't the style in America. I came down one morning from the room Jack and I shared in the attic, and Brina looked at me and said, "Look what she is wearing!" As in "How pathetic! How scandalous that she should be dressed this way." The current style, it turned out, was just the opposite of what I had on—pencil skirts, everything tight to the body and trim. I was out of fashion. This was apparently intolerable. Kindly Mannes suggested a correction.

Brina and I set out for a day in town. I was nervous to go out with her; I didn't know what to expect. I was thoroughly in her power; I didn't know my way about the town, and I didn't yet know any English. But, still, I was excited by the prospect—the idea of going into a store, with money to spend; the idea of looking around at the items for sale; to pick up, maybe, a hat, a pair of gloves; to try something on and look at myself in the mirror. These simple pleasures in life, these girlish delights—they had been lost to me for so long. I was happy at the idea of a little adventure.

We went first to a shoe and hosiery shop. Brina was known there, as she was known throughout Beacon. The proprietor greeted her warmly, and Brina introduced me as if I were a charity case, a pathetic creature from another world: I was her "greener." That became Brina's standard descriptor of both me and Jack—her "greeners," her greenhorns. The term had such condescension in it; it was so breezily dismissive, so cavalier: a greenhorn—someone ignorant, someone foreign, maybe not quite human. The word—it's the same in Yiddish as in English—comes from the Middle Ages; it refers to a young cow whose undeveloped horns are still green.

The store owner looked at me with a mixture of pity and dismay. I felt awkward and embarrassed, but I was angered, too, that Brina had presented me as if I were a pauper. The man must have understood Brina's meaning, because he went to the back and got several pairs of stockings to give me—for free, as a form of charity. It was generous of him, to be sure; but I was mortified. I had no wish to be a charity case.

He handed me the package, I nodded my thanks, and we left.

Woolworth's was next, the local five-and-dime. I remember feeling overwhelmed by the amount of stuff they had for sale—aisle after aisle of household goods, stationery, toiletries—even an aisle for "Sundries," for items that didn't fit into any other category. Brina bought some things and handed me the bag to carry for her on our walk home.

It's not that I minded the carrying so much; I would have been happy to carry a package for her if she had asked. But she didn't ask; she presumed—as if the whole reason for my being there, for being out with her shopping was so that I could carry the packages for her.

When we got home, she took the bags from me—both the one from the hosiery shop and the one from Woolworth's—and she kept the contents, stockings and all, for herself.

I began to realize that I was her maid. I had come to America to be Brina's maid.

One afternoon, I sat outside to take a little rest in the sun. Brina called to me from the kitchen: "Malka, come here." Dutifully, I came in and saw her sitting at the table grinding meat. She said, "Malka, here: grind this meat for me." No need for pleasantries, no need for warmth, no need to ask, might I please. . . . I was her servant, not a guest, not a member of her family.

I grew frightened of her.

She served dinner every night in meager portions—maybe two or three ounces of meat, a half of a potato. It couldn't have been the cost of the food that was dictating the size of her meals; she and Mannes had enough money to feed as many people as they chose. Maybe they were already involved in the American way of endless dieting—I don't know. But even if the portions were enough for them, who for years had already had so much, they never seemed sufficient to us; they never were able to satisfy our constant hunger. I was pregnant, and Jack's nephew, Sidney, was a young man of eighteen. Surrounded by abundance, we were always hungry.

One evening, after dinner was over and everyone had retired for the night, Jack and Sidney decided to go down to the kitchen and get some toast so the three of us could quietly take another few bites of food before we went to bed. I thought they'd bring back three slices, one for each of us. But when they returned, I saw they had with them seven or eight slices— maybe half a loaf of bread—and I got scared. We couldn't possibly take all that bread for ourselves; Brina would notice that the bread was gone the next morning, and she would accuse us of stealing. I refused to eat anything until they agreed to bring back down to the kitchen half of what they had taken.

Would she really have accused me of stealing? Was she really that coldhearted? Perhaps not, but all I got from her was icy disdain and the glance of someone who despised me.

One day, Brina showed me a boxful of pictures. They were from her youth in Radom, and they showed groups of people, some young, standing arm in arm or sitting on benches outside buildings, some older, standing formally as if for a portrait. The photographs were black and white, grainy, as all pictures were in those days, and I didn't recognize anyone in them. Brina was at least thirty years older than I; it would have been unlikely for me to know anyone she knew in Radom. But then, in one picture, I noticed a man I recognized—Ydel Weissman, who had been a friend of my brother's.

"Him," I said, pointing to the picture, "I know him. That's Ydel Weissman."

"That's my sister's husband," she replied. "So tell me now why you survived and my sister didn't."

It was an accusation, not a question.

I couldn't stay in Beacon; the place was intolerable to me. I told Jack we had to go. I would work, of course; I would be happy to clean houses, to scrub floors. This didn't bother me; I wasn't afraid to work. But not for her, not for Brina, not in Beacon.

Jack agreed; he, too, felt uncomfortable there. So we told Mannes and Brina that we'd be going—"Yes," Brina said, "yes, New York is a much better place for a young couple to be"— and we left. They didn't ask where we were going; they didn't offer to lend us any money. We were immigrants without any English; we had barely a small suitcase between us; we had no place to go and almost no cash. We had brought with us from

Germany a cigarette case and a small gold ring, intending at first to give them to Mannes and Brina to thank them for their hospitality, but when Jack saw what the situation was, he suggested we keep them for ourselves instead; we also had a Leica camera. These were all our currency; this was all we had to build a life.

We took the train to Manhattan.

17

MARTIN WAS BORN ON FEBRUARY 11, 1947. JACK AND I brought him back from the hospital ten days later. I had a difficult delivery, and after twenty-four hours of labor, Martin had to be delivered by forceps. But I was so happy to have given birth, and to a healthy child. I had been worried that the baby might come out looking a little like a monkey—I had been to the zoo at some point over the summer, and I had watched the monkeys playing in their dark cages. Received wisdom in those days (and how was I to know any different? Who did I have to tell me otherwise?) was that if a pregnant woman saw something out of the ordinary—and to me, of course, monkeys were surely out of the ordinary—then the image of whatever she saw would likely get imprinted on her baby. Babies born with what used to be called harelips were said to be born that way because their mothers, while pregnant, had probably looked at rabbits. I worried that my baby might not come out right, because of the monkeys. But Martin was perfect: ten tiny fingers and ten tiny toes, and an impossibly silken head and the softest blue eyes. We brought him back to our apartment and tucked him into the little bed we had made with a pillow and some towels inside a dresser drawer. I was a mother, young and terrified.

Essentially, Jack and I were squatters in a mostly abandoned building down by the Williamsburg Bridge on the Lower East Side. We had moved there after spending several months renting a couple of rooms from Jack's cousin Molly. We had sold the Leica camera we brought with us from Europe—we told the man in the camera shop to pay us whatever he thought the camera was worth, and he gave us seventy-five dollars, which, we later found out, was much less than it was worth, but to us at that time it was a real fortune—and we paid Molly seventeen dollars a month rent. But by early fall, we realized that we needed a place of our own and we had heard that on the Lower East Side, you could live pretty much anywhere you wanted.

The building on Lewis Street where we set up house had been abandoned by its landlord after it was condemned by the Board of Health. The place had electricity and cold running water, but no heat or hot water. Garbage piled up on the street outside the building, and the smell of rotting waste rose up and into the apartments. I chose an apartment on the third floor of the walk-up to try to get away from the stench.

In the winter, when we brought Martin home, we could never get warm enough. With no heat, we slept in as many layers of clothes as we could put on—three pair of socks, shirts and sweaters, scarves and hats. We bundled up like hobos.

There was a bathtub in the center of the kitchen, and during the summer, I would fill it with cold water so I could take a soak to try to cool off. One night, I tried sleeping on the fire escape to get a little air, but I was scared of the animals that might come in the night so I came back inside.

The place was primitive, and I cried to think that this, too, was America—this filth, this poverty, the garbage and the stink and the wind thrashing at the windows—but the place was ours. It was my first home, my first real home, since I had to move with my family to the ghetto six years before. I was determined to make it as lovely as I possibly could. I scrubbed the floors with vinegar and salt; I scoured the sink and lined the cupboard shelves with paper. I bought fabric on Orchard Street and made little curtains for the windows. It was a squatter's apartment, truly, but it felt almost like a little household. Jack found work in the garment district; my father and Sidney eventually moved into another apartment on the same floor. I kept the place clean and I made dinner every night, and when we brought Martin home from the hospital and tucked him into the little bed inside a drawer, it really did feel as if we had made a family. Our very own home, our very own son.

I was scared all the time.

I had no idea how to care for a child. An old woman lived down the hall—a stooped and sorry creature she was, but she

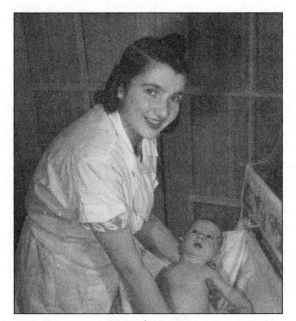

Me with Martin

became my guide because I had no one else to guide me. Martin scratched himself just slightly on his face, and this woman told me I had to cut his nails. But how could I take a pair of scissors to fingers so impossibly small? How would I hold him still? She told me I had to be very careful about germs, that germs were all about and that germs could make Martin sick. So everything Martin wore—his little shirts, his pants, his socks, his diapers—I washed in boiling water, dried them, and ironed them. I ironed every one of Martin's clean diapers to kill the germs that may have lurked there.

I was worried he wouldn't talk. He was a very good baby, undemanding and easily settled. He didn't cry much, but it never occurred to me that his soft gurglings could be a sign of contentment. Instead, I fretted. "How will he talk if he doesn't cry?" Knowing nothing about these things, I brought him to a clinic and told the doctor what was worrying me. The doctor snatched the bottle from Martin's mouth and started to tease him, bringing the bottle back close to his lips and then pulling it away before Martin could latch on. The poor child started to wail within seconds. "See?" the doctor said, "the child can cry just fine."

But I didn't know. I was not yet twenty years old, and I had no one to teach me, no one to encourage me and tell me not to be anxious. No one to tell me I was doing a good job. Jack tried to be supportive, of course, but he knew even less than I. He was fearful, too—he wouldn't even hold Martin for fear of dropping him. I loved being a mother; it satisfied something deep inside me, some longing to be infinitely attached to another living being. But I couldn't enjoy it as much as I wanted to. I was busy all the time with the diapers and the cleaning, and more than that, I was afraid, daunted by the worry that I wouldn't do things right. It wasn't just the practicalities, making sure Martin was safe and clean and healthy, making sure he ate enough, hoping he was growing enough, and watching that he wouldn't stumble on the stairs as he started to walk. It was the dream. That dreadful dream.

Even after my daytime fears began to fade, after I began to learn to trust my own sense of how to be a mother, of how to raise a child, even after our second son, David, was born three years later, and I wasn't any longer so worried about how to bathe a child or how to hold him when his nails needed to be clipped, after I even stopped ironing clean diapers, still the dream came. For years and years, long after we moved from Lewis Street and settled into a series of ever-nicer apartments, the dream followed me like a demon. My children grew into adolescence and then into adulthood, and still the dream would wake me in the night, and I would find myself cold and clammy at once, my heart racing.

In the dream, I am in Auschwitz.

At some point, fairly early on in my time in Auschwitz, before Mima stole the pair of children's shoes for me—this part is true, this part isn't dream—all the women in our group, the ammunition workers from Radom, were moved from one part of the camp to another, as I have said. I was still wearing those murderous wooden clogs. The ground around the new barracks was covered with jagged stones. Not packed dirt, not gravel, but large stones covered the ground, stones with sharp edges, as if new and roughly hewn from a quarry. It was hard to walk over these stones; there was no place to get a secure footing among all the uneven edges. The wooden clogs—with no give to them, with no way to accommodate the ups and downs of the irregular shapes—made it harder still. Sometimes I fell—a few times I fell just trying to walk across the yard—and falling was dangerous: If you fell at the wrong time, if the wrong person saw you fall, you could get beaten, or killed.

It is this scene that comes to me in the dream. I am back there, in that yard in Auschwitz, wearing those wicked wooden clogs, standing precariously on those jagged stones. In the dream, it's just like it was then, only now it's worse—because now I'm holding Martin. He's a small child—maybe just a year old—and he doesn't yet know how to walk. He's not wearing any shoes, so he couldn't walk, anyway, if I put him down. But I can't put him down, because he'll try to crawl if I do, and if he crawls in this place, if he lays those lovely knees, those dimpled hands, down on those stones, then his supple skin, his skin softer than the softest eiderdown, will get cut. Those rocky points, those jagged edges, will dig into Martin's skin and make him bleed. In the dream, I hold him; I cannot put him down. The sun is baking the stones, and the heat rises thick and heavy in front of me. My arms are straining under the weight of my poor boy, caught with me in this camp, with nowhere to go. I am holding him—my God! I am holding him—as I must. Yet my arms are on fire with his huge heaviness, with the load of my lovely and beloved boy. I must hold my son, I must keep him clasped to me, but I feel my grip failing. I feel my son starting to fall.

This is the dream. I told it once to a German psychiatrist—back in the 1950s, the German government sent me to doctors and to a psychiatrist in New York when it was working out its reparations to survivors—and the psychiatrist who heard my dream told me he thought it was "fascinating." Then he advised me to put the past behind me and get on with my life.

Jack would try to comfort me when I awoke from the dream. He would hold me, and I would cry in his arms, and he would make a little joke about something as he always did, and I would eventually find my way back to sleep.

I don't dream the dream so much anymore. But sometimes I do. Sometimes it returns, vivid and visceral as ever. And then I am again in Auschwitz, fearful of taking even a single step.

Epilogue

I AM OLD NOW; THERE'S NO DENYING THAT. MY SKIN IS translucent, like tissue paper; I can see my veins down the underside of my arms. My hair, baby fine to begin with, thinned out nearly to nothingness decades ago. I had a small stroke a few years back, and sometimes now I'm unsteady on my feet, but I am determined to walk without a cane.

It's hard to be alone. I have friends who are on their own now, widows after decades of marriage. Somehow they seem to manage, though truly I can't say what they feel deep down, in the quiet of their nights. I know for me, it is hard—really, I think, unbearably hard. I don't understand why life is set up this way, why one partner should die and leave the other all alone. True partners should die together, at one and the same time.

I loved Jack, and I loved the life we worked so hard to create. We built a business over decades: Jack and I made all the financial decisions together; I did a lot of the labor on my own. In the early years, even with two small children to care for, I cleaned apartments and saw to their furnishing, and I would travel often by subway and almost always at night to collect rent payments from our tenants. I wasn't afraid; I had been through worse. Jack and I were trying to make something of ourselves, for ourselves and for our family, and we were doing it together, as partners.

I always put Jack first, before myself, certainly—even before the children. I wanted to make him happy, to make up as best I could for all he had suffered in the war. I made lunch for him every day and helped him with his coat and handed him his briefcase as he left for work every morning. He was scared to drive, so I drove him everywhere—to his business appointments, to lunch meetings, to the barber. We were always together.

In turn, I know, Jack always wanted to indulge me. He could never take me on enough vacations—to spas in Italy, especially, where we would get massages and lounge in thick cotton robes during the days and eat fancy meals at night— and he could never buy me enough gifts. Eventually, I stopped saying that I admired something—a piece of jewelry, perhaps, or a vase or a figurine—if we were taking a walk and looking in shop windows, because always the next day, I would find whatever it was I had pointed to wrapped up for me in a pretty box. Even as I grew into middle age and put on a few pounds, Jack never wanted me to diet; he said I was beautiful just as I was, and besides, hadn't I suffered enough starvation during the war?

Jack answered the question I had asked myself at the moment of my liberation—to whom do I belong, and who belongs to me? For sixty years, Jack and I belonged to each other. I can't imagine what my life would have been without him. Mima told me in Garmisch-Partenkirchen that I would be safe with Jack, and she was right.

Others kept me safe, too, of course, before Jack. In telling my story, I have wanted very much to honor them—Mima and Feter, Zwirek and Zosia, Katz and Leon Rosenbaum, and a German man whose name I never knew. The thought of these selfless souls has comforted and sustained me over the years. Family and strangers, Jews and Gentiles, these simple people were simply good to me, though I had done nothing to deserve their goodness and though I could never pay them back. If I don't so much believe in God anymore, I do believe in people: I believe that even in the most horrendous circumstances, there is still space for choice. No matter what the situation, people still get to determine how they will be in the world—whether good or evil, kind or cruel, or anything in between—through daily acts of choice, both large and small. Mima and Feter, Zwirek and Zosia, and all the rest of them— they made choices that helped me live when so many others did not.

I want the world to know about these people, these quiet heroes of my life.

Most of all, though, I want the world to know about Heniek, who never got to build a family to honor and remember him. I don't want Heniek to be erased from history; I want to give Heniek his due, for he chose to be a kind and gentle man in the very worst of times. For sixty-five years, I have kept Heniek to myself. The picture Mima preserved in her shoe, creased in the middle and flaking at the edges, and the golden rings that Jadzia Fetman hid—these have been my private tokens. Every now and then—sometimes once a month, sometimes more—I go to my closet, reach back behind the folded sweaters and neatly stacked boxes of scarves, and retrieve my rings and my picture from their hiding place. Then for a few moments, I sit by myself and hold the rings in my hand and gaze at the picture, our two faces so graceful in their youth, so seemingly unspoiled, and remember again the feeling of what Heniek and I shared—that first kiss, that aching desire, those few brief weeks of hope. To know, secretly, that I was once that girl, that young girl Heniek chose to be his bride . . .

ﻙﻷ

It is hard to be old, but there's something liberating about old age, too, because finally you realize that you can claim your history in all its fullness, that you can give voice to your memory and speak its truth, and that it is not a betrayal or an indiscretion to do so.

Now I am done with secrets. Now I claim my first love, lest it die with me:

My Heniek, I loved you so.

MILLIE WERBER is today the matriarch of a close and loving family. After moving to the United States in 1946, she and her husband Jack raised their two sons in Queens, New York, where together they built a real estate business. They lived happily together for 60 years until Jack's death in 2006. Millie now lives on Long Island surrounded by her children, grand-children, and great-grandchildren.

EVE KELLER is Professor of English and Director of Graduate Studies in the English Department of Fordham University. Author of *Generating Bodies and Gendered Selves: The Rhetoric of Reproduction in Early Modern England*, she has published widely on the literature, science, and medicine of early modern England. She lives in suburban New York with her husband, two children, and a hedgehog.

4/12